ILNER FIELD

THE LOST COUNTRY HOUSE OF

TITUS SALT Jnr

This edition first published in 2011 by
Barleybrook Ltd.
Printed by Gomer Press Limited,Wales.

Milner Field : The Lost Country House of Titus Salt Jnr was first published in 2011 by
Barleybrook Ltd. Copyright © Richard Lee-Van den Daele and R David Beale.
Book design and layout © David Weber.

British Library Cataloguing in Publication Data.
A catalogue record for this book is available from the British Library.

In producing this book every reasonable effort has been made to obtain the necessary
permissions for photographic illustrations, documents, etc.

ISBN 978-0-9569380-0-8

Frontispiece : Bookplate belonging to Titus Salt Jnr.

Design and book layout by David Weber
Cover design and Milner Field floor plan by Terry Medhurst
Typeset in 11/14 TNR
Published by Barleybrook Ltd
Printed and bound by Gomer Press Ltd

Quid non Deo juvante

Titus Salt Junr

Acknowledgments

As with any work of this type, our efforts would have been severely hindered without the help and encouragement of a vast number of people. The gestation period of this book has been, of necessity, a long one and we would like to offer our apologies to anyone who has assisted us and is not mentioned here.

This book would have been much the poorer without the invaluable help of two members of the Salt family – Denys and Nick. They have freely given us access not only to the private archive of papers and memorabilia relating to their family's association with the village which bears their name, but have also been generous with family anecdotes, points of correction and much other fine detail. In similar vein, Richard and the late Anne Trist have offered unfailing support and made available to us the wonderful cache of family photographs relating to the tenure of the Hollins family at Milner Field. Mrs Dorothy Burrows of Shipley, Richard D. Hirst, the National Archives, the Scottish Ironwork Foundation, Mr Mervyn Adams of BKS Surveys Ltd, Sue Hills of the Strathallen Castle Archive and John Irwin were also generous with their photographs.

For his tireless help, boundless enthusiasm and great insight we are hugely indebted to David Weber. Dave Shaw, Kathryn Ross and Philip Barlow have also been generous with their time and knowledge and we greatly appreciate their support. Carol Greenwood, her successor, and staff at the Bradford Central Library Local Studies Department and those of the West Yorkshire Archive Service offered much help, as did those at Shipley & Bingley libraries.

The late Clive Woods of Saltaire Village Society, Julie Woodward of Shipley College, Allan Mirfield, Eugene Nicholson and his colleagues at the Bradford Industrial Museum, Dr Adam White of Lotherton Hall, Ian Watson of Saltaire History Club, Helen Mills of Bingley Local History Society, Brenda Armstrong, Stephen Whitehead, Daru Rooke, Ian Jones, David King, Dale Keeton and Christine Hopper of Bradford Libraries & Museums Service were also of great assistance. Similarly our correspondence with Mary Tetlow, Donald Hanson, Harry Downs, Peter Horne, Barry Wood, Ken Eastell, P. Barry F. Whitaker, Bill Tegner and Stephen Gautrey was never less than fascinating and our thanks go to them also.

Numerous individuals with recollections of the house gave their time to be interviewed and principal among these we wish to offer sincere thanks to Bob MacDonald, Trevor Meek, the late Richard Hollins, MBE, Norman Firth, Eric Smith, the late Eric Scrivener and Arthur Moorby.

Lastly, we are indebted to our families who have borne this long project with goodwill and tolerance and whose comments on the text have invariably been constructive.

Richard Lee-Van den Daele and R David Beale
Shipley
Summer 2011

CONTENTS

Authors' note: In order to avoid confusion, throughout the book Titus Salt senior is referred to as 'Sir Titus' and Titus Salt junior as 'Titus Jnr'.

Foreword by
Denys Salt

It is with particular pleasure and personal pride that I warmly commend this fascinating account of one of the great Yorkshire houses, now sadly demolished, to the reader.

For it was my grandfather, Titus Salt Jnr who, on his marriage to Catherine Crossley, with considerable artistic discernment and generous financial endowment employing all that was best in construction, decoration, landscaping and technological innovation, built an impressive mansion as a family home that perfectly reflected the affluence and taste of his day. This is also where my father Harold, his two brothers Gordon and Lawrence and sister Isabel all spent their childhoods.

In this publication can be found full descriptions of the interior of the house and gardens and of the life surrounding them in clear life-like terms.

On two separate occasions Milner Field was the setting for Royal Visits on an elaborate scale, meticulously stage-managed in a Salt/Crossley partnership, with my grandmother clearly relishing her role as a society hostess.

But the house also had a darker side to its history and its changing fortunes over the years have been admirably portrayed, with skill and perception, painstakingly supported by much contemporary research, by the joint authors, Richard Lee-Van den Daele and R David Beale. The book's attractive design and great pictorial impact owes much to the skill of David Weber.

When one considers how many fine country houses have been lost through demolition and other causes in the course of the past century, it is indeed refreshing and rewarding to be presented with such an authentic chronicle of one such house and its successive occupants over the years.

Denys Salt

Introduction

A neglected pathway leads from the end of Baildon's Coach Road past a solitary gatehouse and is darkened, on even the brightest of days, by an impenetrable canopy of overhanging trees. The stillness and solitude are scarcely broken. Few visitors to this densely overgrown area would realise they were treading the carriage drive to Milner Field, one of the area's finest country houses built by the son of perhaps its most influential industrialist.

Milner Field, Ferniehurst and The Knoll are all names which, to the historically-minded in the Saltaire and Baildon district, conjure up the elegance and genteel living of a vanished age.

Fig 1: Architectural sketch of Milner Field, "The Builder" March 15th 1873.

Two of these grand nineteenth century mansions - Milner Field and Ferniehurst - were built by the sons of Sir Titus Salt, and came to epitomise the wealth and social pre-eminence of the Salt family.

Now all three houses have been swept away and barely a vestige remains to recall their grandeur. Yet the Salts, caught like insects in amber, reveal themselves best in their domestic setting.

Figs 2, 3 & 4: Sir Titus Salt chose Crow Nest at Lightcliffe near Halifax as his home. Originally renting the house, he finally purchased it in 1867 and lived there until his death in 1876.

Over the years much has been written about Sir Titus Salt and the Italianate mill village, with its institute, hospital and schools together with church and rows of workers' stone dwellings, which bears his name. Surprisingly little attention though has been paid to the houses the family themselves occupied. Unlike some of his sons, Sir Titus did not live close to the Salt 'palace of industry', though he had apparently considered building a mansion and laying out a park near the bottom of Fairbank Wood on the north side of the river Aire[1]. He did not however do so, though his partner Mr Charles Stead did build the Knoll in 1858 on the hilltop nearby.

Fig 5: The Knoll, seen from Saltaire park.

Instead Sir Titus made his home at Crow Nest at Lightcliffe, some four miles from Halifax and six miles from Bradford. He rented the house from 1844 to 1858, only somewhat reluctantly leaving when the owner, Mr E. C. Sutherland-Walker, needed to occupy it himself. Sir Titus moved to Methley Park in the interim and returned as the owner of Crow Nest and its eighty two acre park following an abortive auction in 1867 and resided there until his death on 29th December 1876. During his occupancy tremendous celebrations to mark his fifty third birthday took place on 20th September 1856, to which he invited all his employees. Their amusement at viewing the angoras, llamas and alpacas roaming the grounds, or inspecting the banana trees Sir Titus grew, can only be guessed at. This gathering was only to be eclipsed by a massive party he held there in 1873 to mark his seventieth birthday and the twentieth anniversary of the opening of the mill to which no fewer than 4,200 guests were invited, many being conveyed there on specially-scheduled trains.

After Sir Titus' death his executors sold Crow Nest in 1878 to another mill owner, Richard Kershaw, and the house remained a family home until Kershaw's death in 1917. Interestingly, the taste for socialising on a lavish scale must have persisted in the tenure of Sir Titus' successor, as the six-day sale which followed Kershaw's death recorded the sale of 500 bottles of vintage port. Sadly, eighteenth century Crow Nest - like the other Salt houses, including

Fig 6: Occasions of celebration allowed the Victorians to indulge their love of finery and elegance.

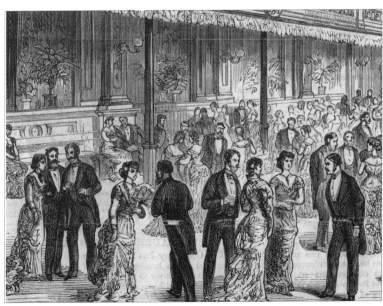

Methley Hall near Wakefield - has long since been demolished, robbing the historian of the opportunity to explore the domestic world of the wealthy and titled landowner.

We would like to briefly examine how we came to lose so many historically and architecturally notable buildings during the course of the last seventy or eighty years.

By the middle of the twentieth century, the future of the English country house was uncertain. A large and outmoded mansion, set in sprawling parkland, had become a luxury few could still afford. Enormous maintenance costs and crippling death duties were other factors which left many owners facing a drastic course of action: demolition.

Fig 7: Sir Titus was unusual but not exceptional in his philanthropic ideals, but few if any mill owners would extend an invitation to their entire workforce, as he did.

In Milner Field's case, though it was no longer the sole possession of an eminent family forced to live in reduced circumstances, the problems besetting so many country houses throughout Britain weighed just as surely against it.

Fig 8: Milner Field shared the fate of many grand country houses. This rare picture from the 1950s shows the roofless house well on its way to complete dereliction.

In 1946 at least two thousand once magnificent country houses dotted the English countryside; neglected, riddled with damp and dry rot, and awaiting the inescapable arrival of sledgehammer and pickaxe. The author and architectural historian John Harris has calculated that by 1955 a country house was being demolished, somewhere in England, every two and a half days. He likens the loss in architectural terms alone to be *"probably as great as that from the destructions following the Dissolution of the Monasteries"*[2].

The pervading sense of despair felt by the owners was exacerbated by a society which, through twenty-first century eyes, seems initially to be wanton in its appetite for destruction. Placing the situation in context, as Harris does, throws into relief the beleaguered position that many owners faced: "*Even if there had been any awareness that a valuable heritage was being destroyed, there were few means of rescue: no amenity societies concerned with the problem, no National Trust, no state grants, no developed tourism - and apart from schools, private mental homes and some local authority adaptations, there were few alternative uses*"[3]. A similarly hopeless predicament was to face the Salts company who latterly owned Milner Field as their two unsuccessful attempts to auction off the property testify.

Milner Field, a product of more affluent times, was decidedly unfashionable by the 1920s. Rambling, difficult to heat and assailed by damp, the house was to meet a fate not dissimilar to that engulfing many houses right across the nation. As we shall explore, at Milner Field the eventual destruction was not driven solely by practical considerations: the house had gained a grim reputation locally and the series of misfortunes which befell its occupants compounded the dilemma facing its owners.

Fig 9: Titus Salt Jnr.

That Milner Field met its end at the hands of a demolition gang is in little doubt, but its final years and the exact nature of its destruction still remain something of a mystery.

West Yorkshire boasted a great number of fine houses and the captains of the burgeoning Victorian textile industry lost no time in erecting homes reflecting their new station in life.

Fig 10: Catherine Salt, née Crossley.

Fig 11: Baildon Lodge in 2009.

Edward Salt erected Ferniehurst and the story of this magnificent house is touched on later in this book. Titus Salt Jnr chose a site with majestic views overlooking the Aire Valley for his home, though he enjoyed its comforts for a mere fourteen years.

Titus Salt Jnr was born on 28th August 1843, the fifth and youngest surviving son of Sir Titus Salt and Lady Caroline. By the age of twenty-two he had become involved in the family textile manufacturing business and his ready grasp of the principles and strategies necessary to succeed astounded those who observed him. A dynastic marriage to Catherine Crossley, daughter of Halifax carpet baron Joseph Crossley, followed on 15th March 1866. The couple honeymooned in Venice and in Switzerland.

By his mid twenties Titus Jnr's aesthetic tastes were sufficiently well-developed to result in his commissioning costly furniture, made to exacting designs by Charles Bevan, for the home he shared with his wife at Baildon Lodge, which to this day stands in Station Road, Baildon (Fig 11). His 1866 bill from Marsh and Jones, the exclusive firm of Leeds cabinet makers, totalled in excess of £4,000. As an interesting comparison, at that time a scullery maid earned about £12 a year.

Fig 12: The Elizabethan Milner Field, seen here in the 1860s prior to its demolition by Titus Jnr.

Old Milner Field

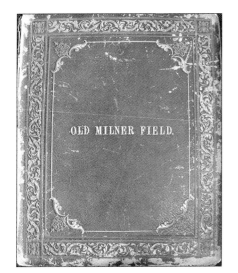

Fig 13: Titus Jnr's leather bound history of old Milner Field.

Nine months after their marriage, while the young couple still lived in the well-appointed but more modest surroundings of Baildon Lodge, *The Bradford Observer* carried an advertisement inviting offers for the Milner Field and Stubbing House estates near Bingley. The plot comprised the *"fine old mansion called Milner Field, with the coach-houses, stables ... two farm-houses, a cottage and about 161 acres of rich arable, meadow, pasture and woodland "*[4].

The manorial lands known as Milner Field enjoyed a long and distinguished history, with three eminent local families - the Milners, the Oldfields and the Fells - having laid successive claim to the area. It is unclear when the first building was erected on the site, though an inscription on the first recorded dwelling house, which Titus Jnr was to later demolish, showed that it had been built - or possibly rebuilt - by John Oldfield in 1603.

Titus Jnr was evidently proud of the land's impressive history, as he retained the commemorative stone bearing this date and the monograms of Oldfield and his wife and, together with the pair of monumental ball finial gateposts, incorporated them into the new building and its gardens. It is probable that the 1877 history of old Milner Field (Fig 13) – still in the Salt family's personal archives, bound in morocco leather and fronted by a beautiful plate of the Elizabethan manor house (Fig 15), was commissioned by Titus Jnr himself.

Nineteenth century local historian, Harry Speight, gives us this glimpse inside the manorial house Salt was to pull down: *"It was a roomy old place, the ground floor consisting of only two compartments, with a decidedly Tudor look about them. The large hall had a gallery running around it in the old Elizabethan style,*

Fig 14: The gateposts of old Milner Field in 1930.

13

Fig 15: Old Milner Field c1860, showing the pair of ivy clad gateposts and retaining wall which Titus Jnr was to incorporate in the grounds of his new house.

one side of which gave access to the bedrooms, while another small part was raised as if it had been intended to serve the purpose of a rostrum from which to address those assembled around or below"[5].

The house itself, probably owing to its then somewhat neglected state, does not seem to have been well-regarded by another local (and later very prominent) figure. The educational reformer, William Forster, had apparently considered purchasing the house and estate himself and a visit to the site was recorded in the diary of his friend Barclay Fox. Fox states that he *"spent the day quietly with William, riding together to Milner Field, a place he is tempted to take as a residence. I discouraged it. The house is a tempting old hall, enough to set off the imagination; but it will require much repairing and fitting up. It is five miles from Bradford and the road is very bad"[6].*

Fig 16: Line drawing of old Milner Field.

14

Fig 17: Above. Barry's Palace of Westminster.
Fig 18: Right. Lockwood and Mawson's Bradford
Town Hall, opened in September 1873.

The house changed hands several times before eventually passing in 1834 to John Wilmer Field of Heaton Hall for £8,000. On his death in about 1839 his daughters inherited the estate. The younger daughter, who was married to Admiral Arthur Duncombe, eventually sold the land to the Salt family in 1869 for £21,000.

At the time of the purchase, the Elizabethan tastes the old house embodied were becoming less highly regarded as the Gothic revival style began to catch the popular imagination. This sea-change in public discernment is perhaps best exemplified by the design competition for the new Palace of Westminster held in 1835, which stipulated that only two styles would be considered - Elizabethan and Gothic. Both styles were thought to be peculiarly British and as such highly appropriate for such an institution. Of the ninety-seven entries received, ninety-one were in the Gothic style.

Charles Barry and A. W. N. Pugin went on to create the new seat of government in a wonderfully unfettered Gothic revival style and, although formally opened in

Fig 19: Methley Hall interior.

1852, the building was not completed until 1867 - just two years before Milner Field was started. Perhaps the most potent image of the building is its pair of towers, one of which is the clock tower housing Big Ben. Titus Jnr's house would also have two towers, one boasting a magnificent quarter-chiming clock with a dark face possibly set with agates, supplied by William Potts & Sons of Leeds. The Salt family had dealt for a number of years with Potts and they had been commissioned to provide the clock for the Congregational Church and had also provided many clocks for their private houses.

If further evidence was needed of the voguish nature of this architectural style, one need look no further than the new Town Hall in Bradford, a building roughly contemporaneous

Fig 20: Milner Field: on which work began in 1869.

with Titus Jnr's house. It was built in the Gothic style by the Bradford architectural practice of Lockwood and Mawson who had designed Saltaire and many of Bradford's other prominent civic buildings. Though more Italianate in flavour than Milner Field, the Town Hall generated a great deal of admiration, not least for its impressive 225 foot high clock tower based on that of the Palazzo Vecchio in Florence. Titus Jnr was naturally familiar with this building, having been a Town Councillor until 1871. He even crafted the ceremonial mallet which was used by the Mayor to lay the foundation stone in August 1870. Interestingly, it has recently come to light that Titus Jnr's architect, Thomas Harris, had on 10th June 1869 expressed an interest in being considered for the design competition initiated for the new Town Hall in Bradford.

Rosemary Claire Saunderson, in her dissertation on Milner Field, *Titus Salt of Milner Field: a study in Nineteenth-century industrialist taste*, asserts that he would have been influenced by styles familiar to him - in particular Methley Hall, the fifteenth century home of the Saviles, Earls of Mexborough. It was the Salt family home from 1858 until 1867 and, according to Balgarnie, was *"built in a castellated style of light stone and adorned with towers and battlements"*[7]. It also housed an impressive Great Hall of painted glass with fine carved woodwork (see Fig 19 of a chromolithograph in the authors' possession).

Fig 21: Two examples of Harris' work. Above: Terraced houses at Harrow c1860. Below: Stokesay Court, a later design from the 1880s.

Building the new Milner Field

Quite why Titus Jnr chose the architect Thomas Harris (1830-1900) to design his new home remains something of a mystery. Harris was far from well-known, in fact Milner Field appears to have been his first large-scale work. He was described by a client as *"a huge shaggy man with a big sombrero hat, rather scraggy beard and tremendous hooked nose, with a deep booming voice [and a tendency to] explode in a rather terrifying way"*[8]. Harris was perhaps better known for his writing than for his designs - it was he who had first coined the phrase "Victorian Architecture" in his book of that title published in 1860. Harris typified the eclectic style of the younger architects of his day (he was thirty-nine when he began work on Milner Field), freely borrowing styles and themes from a wide range of periods and seamlessly blending them into a cohesive whole. He thought the English had, for two hundred and fifty years, *"been doomed to grope about among a chaos of styles"*[9] until the Gothic revival had replaced alien foreign forms with what was felt to be a traditional English style. *"The Architecture of all past ages must be thoughtfully studied"* he wrote in 1860, *"but a reproduction of any of these in this age (advanced as it certainly is in civilisation and scientific knowledge)...will not suffice; no remodelling or adapting will do, but....an indigenous style of our own"*[10].

Nor was Harris a local man, based at Holborn in Gray's Inn Chambers he was not to design any other notable buildings in the north of England. Titus Jnr was more likely to have been attracted by Harris' radical views.

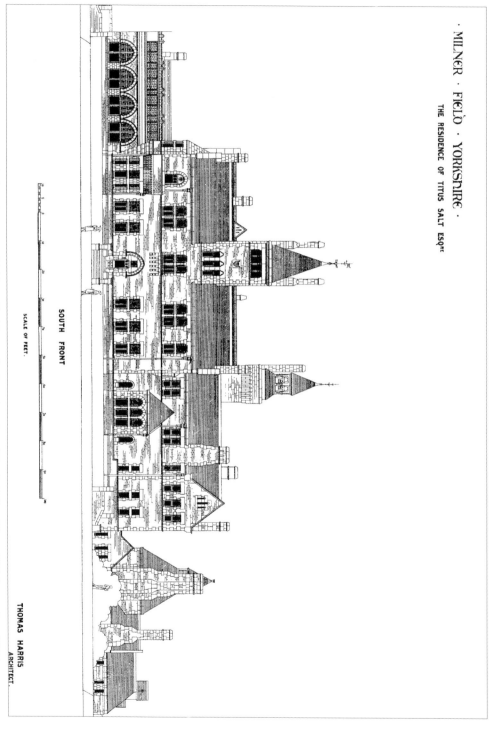

· MILNER · FIELD · YORKSHIRE ·

THE RESIDENCE OF TITUS SALT ESQ.ʳᵉ

SOUTH FRONT

SCALE OF FEET.

THOMAS HARRIS
ARCHITECT.

Fig 22: Architectural plan drawing of Milner Field, south elevation from The Building News 25th December 1874. The kitchen wing can be seen on the right.

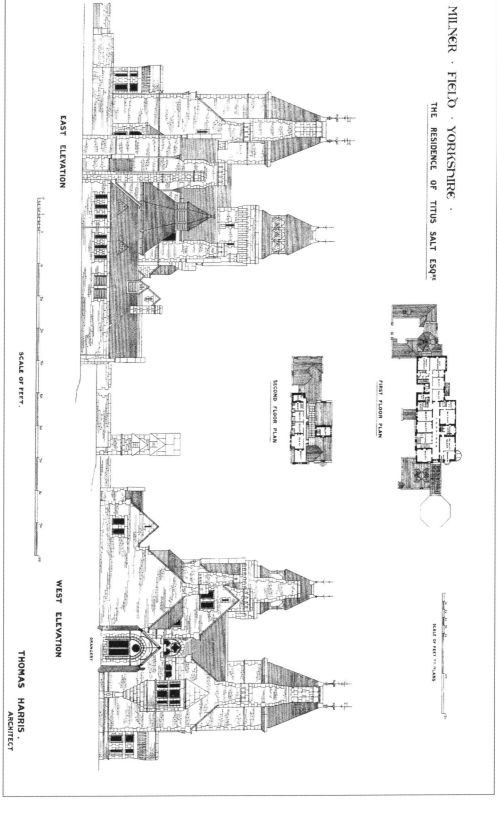

MILNER · FIELD · YORKSHIRE ·

THE RESIDENCE OF TITUS SALT ESQ.RE

EAST ELEVATION

SCALE OF FEET.

FIRST FLOOR PLAN

SECOND FLOOR PLAN

SCALE OF FEET TO PLANS

WEST ELEVATION

ORANGERY

THOMAS HARRIS,
ARCHITECT

Fig 23: East and west elevations.

19

Like Titus Jnr, he was a man of vision and he championed the use of modern materials like iron in the construction of new buildings. *"This is an age of new creations"* stated Harris in his book of 1860, *"steam power and electric communication [are] entirely new revolutionizing influences. So must it be in Architecture"*[11].

Unfairly, Harris and his work held little appeal for posterity and by the 1940s the august periodicals of the architectural profession were attempting to rehabilitate him and his all-but-forgotten reputation. Little wonder then that a sale catalogue for Milner Field in 1922 disingenuously described the house as having been *"erected from the plans of ... Norman Shaw"*[12]. Shaw was a far more eminent architect than Harris - Cragside in Northumberland and the New Scotland Yard building on the Thames embankment were among his most prestigious commissions - and, though the house showed some stylistic details similar to those favoured by Shaw, this attribution was certainly false.

In 1885 the author Healcy describes the house as being constructed of *"grey local stone, the outer walls being lined with brick so as to form hollow walls and thereby prevent[ing] the possibility of dampness"*[13]. The house lay due north and south, with the entrance to the north side through a large ivy-clad Gothic gateway leading to an enclosed courtyard. Twin towers were separated by a steeply-pitched roof finished in Whitland Abbey green slating. The principal rooms were sunny and south-facing and led out to a terrace from which a flight of stone steps descended into a landscaped park. The irregular roofline with its towers, gables and lofty chimneystacks lent the house a startlingly dramatic profile. Viewed from any angle it was an imposing building and the drawing room, library and dining room all looked, fittingly, across the Aire Valley to the seat of the Salt business empire. It was in essence an early, if somewhat lavish, example of 'living over the shop'.

The architectural style of the house, which took two years to build, was distinctly at odds with the more florid, Italianate style of the buildings of Saltaire. The model industrial village that Sir Titus had built contained not only the huge mill, but also decent dwellings for his workforce together with some civic buildings. Far removed from the slums occupied by millworkers in nearby Bradford, Saltaire was aesthetically pleasing and the buildings drew on classical styles and were intended to improve the lives and outlooks of its inhabitants. While still popular for civic buildings, the renaissance Venetian style was widely held to be inappropriate for a gentleman's country house and, as we have seen, was rejected by Harris who clearly looked closer to home for his inspiration. By the 1860s, the word "muscular" had begun to creep into the architectural lexicon and it perfectly describes the substantial home designed for Titus Jnr. Clusters of slender spires were nowhere to be found, instead the block-like towers and rather grim, uncompromising facade echoed its owner's no-nonsense

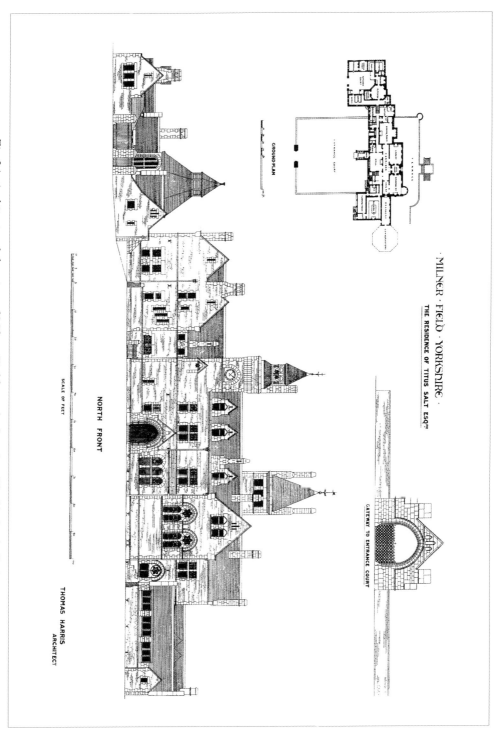

Fig 24: Architectural drawing of Milner Field, north elevation. The kitchen's distinctive octagonal roof and separate gated entrance can be seen on the left.

GROUND-PLAN

· MILNER · FIELD · YORKSHIRE ·

THE RESIDENCE OF TITUS SALT ESQ[RE]

GATEWAY TO ENTRANCE COURT

SCALE OF FEET

NORTH FRONT

THOMAS HARRIS
ARCHITECT

Fig 25: The south face of Milner Field in the mid 1920s, the conical-roofed garden house can be seen in the right foreground.

approach, with little quarter given to the fanciful or merely picturesque. Architectural style had, for Harris, to be truthful. In this he showed himself to be a disciple of Pugin and Ruskin. Buildings created by his fellow architects which simply aped the styles of ancient periods were for him "*nothing more than substantial skeletons, dressed up and disfigured by flimsy shams*". For him, the public "*love for richness and...rage for cheapness, meretricious ornamentation, and expedition at any sacrifice*"[14] held no sway.

The building journals of the day attempted to pigeon-hole the house's look as being in the "Old English" style.

Fig 26: Weekes' panel of medieval peasants: "The Dinner". See also Fig 130.

Fig 27: The only known photograph of the croquet lawn. Situated to the north of the house, the lawn occupied the approximate position of old Milner Field, the gateposts of old Milner Field can be clearly seen. The elderly woman on the left is Bella Foster (mother of Elizabeth Roberts). The odd positioning of the other figures in their wicker chairs is something of a puzzle.

Then, as now, the term alone means little, other than to suggest a style which borrowed architectural motifs somewhat haphazardly and one which could not be safely ascribed to any particular place or period.

The interior of the mansion was no less impressive: reflecting the Gothic taste of the day and executed in a bold, confident manner. Messrs Shaftoe & Barry of York were the general contractors, the wrought iron-work was supplied by Messrs Richardson, Slade & Company of London, while Messrs Burke and Company also of London provided the chimney pieces and marble work. Rosemary Claire Saunderson[15] suggests that Titus Jnr may have been impressed by the work of architect William Burges, which it is likely he would have seen at nearby Oakwood in Bingley (built in 1864). Oakwood was the home of cloth merchant Thomas Garnett, who also hired William Morris and the sculptor Thomas Nicholls who provided the carved decoration. Though Burges never worked personally for Titus Jnr, his master craftsmen were certainly employed by him and he also commissioned Nicholls to work at Milner Field. The richly coloured murals, (Figs 28-30) depicting medieval scenes, and the breathtakingly vivid stained glass panels were created to the designs of Frederick Weekes. The son of sculptor Henry Weekes, Frederick was an accomplished

Fig 28: The Seven Ages of Man, stained glass window by Frederick Weekes. If it survived Milner Field's demolition its current wherebouts are unknown.

Fig 29: Detail from the drawing room fireplace triptych.

Fig 30: Mural of medieval figures from the dining room fireplace.

artist who had exhibited at the Royal Academy in the early 1860s. The stained glass panels were highly regarded at the time, meriting full page illustrations in the *Building News*[16]. *The Dinner*, sited in the dining room, showed medieval peasants gathering food, while in the upper portion of the lancet window overlooking the orangery and conservatory appeared a depiction of Shakespeare's *Seven Ages of Man*. The two panels beneath this were occupied by *Labour* and *Rest*, reinforcing the ubiquitous Victorian work ethic. Weekes was also responsible for the elaborate renaissance panels in the drawing and dining rooms featuring heroic medieval figures, and for the dramatic murals in the billiard room depicting the medieval court and hunt. The lavishly coloured stained glass in the ornate roof presaged the Art Nouveau period and a massive, stepped, white marble fireplace occupied one wall. It is not difficult to imagine the room shrouded with cigar smoke as Titus Jnr and his cronies talked and laughed over a game of billiards.

The kitchens and domestic wing, in common with country houses of the period, were set away from the main body of the house. At Milner Field, the geographical situation lent itself to such a design and the service wing was situated where the land dropped away from the main house. In this way, the undesirable smells and sounds of cooking and laundering would not pervade the principal rooms. The kitchen itself was built in the octagonal Glastonbury style which was popular at the time and based on the famous Abbot's kitchen. Unlike Glastonbury Abbey itself, the Abbot's kitchen is remarkably well-preserved, having survived the ruinous attentions of Henry VIII's men.

Fig 31: Milner Field estate clearly showing the house, conservatory and extensive kitchen gardens, taken in 1922 from 1500 feet.

Fig 32: Aerial view of the estate taken from 1,100 feet in 1922. At the bottom left of the picture stands Oakfield House.

Fig 33: Lawrence, Harold and Gordon Salt, Titus Jnr's three sons enjoying a ride on the miniature railway which served the kitchen garden.

At Milner Field other utilitarian rooms, including water-cooled dairies and larders, were also contained within the kitchen wing which had its own separate gated entrance and courtyard.

The Gardens and Grounds

Titus Jnr had extensive kitchen gardens built on the Primrose Lane side of the estate - the remains of which can be seen to this day - and there were sizeable formal gardens set down by outstanding horticulturalist and landscape garden designer, Robert Marnock. He indulged his love of horticulture by building an enormous conservatory measuring some 3,240 square feet. These winter gardens were positioned at the west end of the house and linked to the drawing room by an orangery. In this way, the semi tropical and exotic plants, along with marble statuary, could be enjoyed from the hall beyond. The glass-enclosed structure was lofty and well-heated and Healey mentions the "*chief objects of notice are the remarkably fine specimens of the tree ferns and palms which are grouped together with striking effect in the centre. One large araucaria reaches nearly to the roof*" – which was nearly 26ft in height! Curious foreign specimens seem to have thrived there. Notable amongst these was the New Zealand flax of which no two leaves were alike in pattern, and an old African fern stump (seven feet high by seven feet in diameter) which culminated in eleven strong crowns of fronds.

The flooring in the conservatory was a mosaic with patterns freely adapted from Roman antiquity. We believe that the remains of the mosaic flooring which can still be seen to this day, though they are now much overgrown with moss and lichen (see Figs 127-128), date from the first decade of the twentieth century when the conservatory underwent extensive remodelling. During the royal visits the Salts hosted, the conservatory was dressed with delicate Chinese lanterns, lending the place an other-worldly charm. On a practical level, Salt incorporated high pressure fire pumps there. He also had other glass and forcing houses built to his own exacting designs and they opened into a covered corridor which allowed each one to be entered without exposing the plants to cold draughts, the added benefit being that all the houses could be visited comfortably whatever the weather. One glasshouse was devoted to growing lapagerias – an evergreen twining climber with glossy dark green leaves whose flowers resemble an exotic tropical orchid and look almost as if carved from wax.

There has been some debate as to the design of the conservatory.

Shown here together for the first time, this series of images indicates that two conservatories occupied the same site.

See also Fig 126.

Fig 34: Top. Salt era photograph showing the original design of the conservatory.

Fig 35: Middle. This image of the ivy clad house with its mature shrubbery shows the original conservatory has been demolished, with only the orangery that led to it, remaining.

Fig 36: Bottom. This and later photographs show the remodelled conservatory with its much more angular porch design. The structures running along the top of the conservatory are a window ventilation system.

As far as the authors are able to ascertain this reconstruction took place during the Roberts' tenure of the property.

Fig 37: The orangery. This covered walkway led from the house to the conservatory, note the added decoration of the chinese lanterns, in place for a royal visit.

Fig 38: Elizabeth Roberts and her grandchildren in the orangery, around 1905. The doorway led into Milner Field's main corridor.

Fig 39: Above. Southern aspect of the greenhouses, the shrubbery archway can be made out in the aerial photograph on Fig 31.

Fig 40: Below. This view gives an indication of the extensive nature of the kitchen gardens at Milner Field.

The plants were trained to cover an arched bower. According to Healey the lapageria alba was "*brought originally from Ferniehurst the house of Mr Edward Salt, which has been stated by competent authorities to be the best plant of its kind in the Kingdom. It extends over a roof space of forty feet and is said to have borne as many as 4,000 flowers at one time*". The range of other forcing houses included hot and cold orchid houses, melon house, fig house, rose house, mushroom house, several peach houses, vineries and gardeners' bothies.

In 1877 the Shipley & Saltaire Times featured a report on the plant houses at Milner Field. The article's un-named author was clearly impressed and stated, "*I know no gardens where the construction of the plant-houses is so obviously in keeping with the notions of the most modern garden architects, if indeed they are not in advance of them*". The author continues, "*immediately to the rear of the winter garden, Mr Salt has, with wise conservation, preserved undisturbed the terrace wall, with steps which formerly led to the old mansion of Milner Field. The site of the house itself is now occupied by a velvety lawn surrounded by a young plantation ... at intervals suggested by the configuration of the ground, specimen trees are placed, which in time will materially contribute to the general effect. The general disposition of the grounds was entrusted to Mr Marnock, a gentleman of great experience in landscape work, who happily had good materials to work upon*". The writer concluded with another paean of praise for Titus Jnr: "*Milner Field may be regarded as affording an apt illustration of the principle that what is worth doing at all is worth doing well*"[17].

Fig 41: The boating lake.

Fig 42: The oak panelled library, featuring one of the elaborate marble fireplaces fitted throughout Milner Field. 1885.

Fig 43: Eastern end of the drawing room (note portière to the right concealing the door of the ante room). 1885.

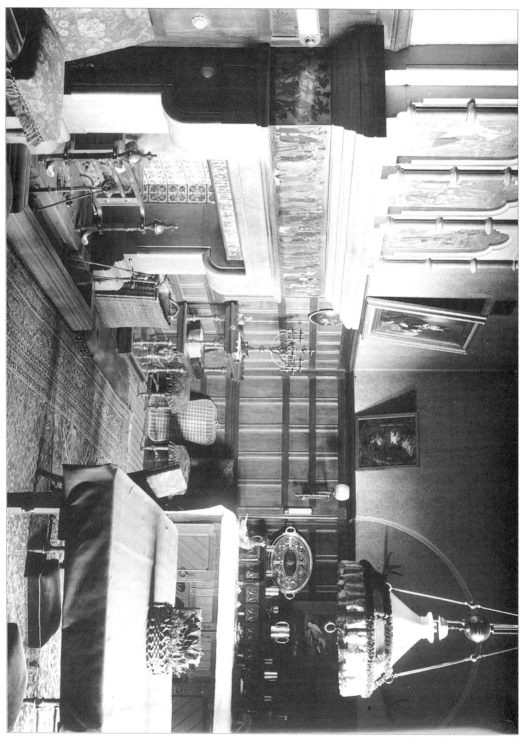

Fig 44: The dining room. Note the triptych mural above the mantlepiece and the ceremonial pageant over the fireplace. 1885.

34

Fig 45: Drawing room, Milner Field. The Victorian love for bric-à-brac is indulged in this busy room. 1885.

The grounds also held a sizeable boating lake which was well-stocked with trout and which was spanned at one end by a rustic bridge. As a leisure pursuit Salt had created a trout hatchery at the house and could provide fish for both the ponds there and at Crow Nest. A small boathouse was erected to one side of the lake (the metal supports for which can still be found in the dense undergrowth) and this provided protection for the handful of pleasure skiffs which the family used on the lake for rowing around the small island in the centre. Harry Speight[18] reported that a bison's tooth was discovered when workmen dug out the lake, shedding some light on the quadrupeds that roamed this part of the county centuries ago.

Fixtures and Fittings

The entrance to the house was reached through an eighteen foot high slate-roofed stone porch which extended seventeen feet into the courtyard. A well-executed pencil sketch of

Figs 46 and 47: Pencil sketches of the Milner Field entrance porch and the south lodge, made in 1887.

the porch, dated March 1887, presumably made as part of the preparations for the second royal visit, along with a drawing of the south lodge and gates are held in the Salt family archive and appear above. Beyond the porch lay the hallway, half-panelled in a mock Jacobean manner. The entrance hall was quite cluttered with furniture in the high Victorian style. A writing desk, gothic armchairs upholstered variously in rich crimson pile and blue Utrecht velvet happily coexisted alongside wicker chairs, bronze urns, fireside companions and a large model of a lifeboat in a glass case. A Fitzroy's Barometer, Japanese waiter (a portable serving table) and a coal hamper completed the scene, while from the walls above the stuffed heads of bison and deer looked down.

A substantial fireplace occupied one wall, while nearby stood the three-manual organ built by Brindley & Foster of Sheffield in the mid-1870s to the family's specifications with both manual and hydraulic power. Titus Jnr's eldest son, Gordon Locksley, was by all accounts an

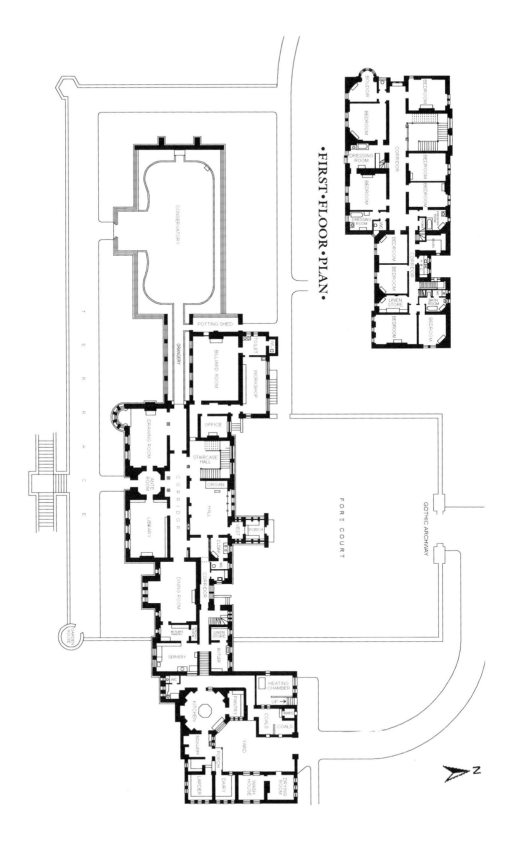

·FIRST·FLOOR·PLAN·

CONSERVATORY

POTTING SHED

TERRACE

ORANGERY

TOILET

WC

BILLIARD ROOM

WORKSHOP

DRAWING ROOM

OFFICE

STAIRCASE HALL

ANTE ROOM

ORGAN

CORRIDOR

HALL

VEST

LIBRARY

CLOAK

PORCH

WC

DINING ROOM

CORRIDOR

GARDEN HOUSE

BUTLERS PANTRY

LINEN STORE

BUTLER

SERVERY

WC

HEATING CHAMBER

UP →

KITCHEN

PANTRY

COALS

ASHES

COALS

SCULLERY

PORCH

YARD

DRYING ROOM

LARDER

DAIRY

WASH HOUSE

FORE COURT

GOTHIC ARCHWAY

N

BOUDOIR

BEDROOM

DRESSING ROOM

BEDROOM

DRESSING ROOM

WC

CORRIDOR

BEDROOM

BEDROOM

BEDROOM

BEDROOM

BEDROOM

CORRIDOR

BEDROOM

LINEN STORE

BATH ROOM

DRESSING ROOM

BEDROOM

BEDROOM

Fig 48: Milner Field Floor Plan.

37

Fig 49: The giant organ dominated the hallway at Milner Field .

accomplished musician and amateur organ builder - he in fact re-registered a number of church organs both in this country and in Northern Ireland - and he must often have played this imposing instrument. Interestingly, in a schedule drawn up by the widowed Catherine Salt before she left the house in 1903, the organ was earmarked for removal, along with some stained glass and the ivory escutcheons and bell pulls which her husband had fashioned (see Fig 50). For some unknown reason though, the organ remained – intriguingly its entry on the schedule is marked by a small pencilled 'x' - and is pictured, accompanied by a glowing description of its virtues, in the sale catalogue of about 1930. The catalogue dates the organ's installation to 1876, though as we see later from Dr Heaton's diary the instrument was certainly in the house in 1875. Its eventual fate, like so much connected with Milner Field, is a mystery.

Leading off the hallway was the drawing room, again half-panelled in oak and with a moulded oak ceiling. Above the panelling was a richly floral patterned paper. Research recently undertaken by Ian Jones points to the paper probably being the William Morris block printed design "Jasmine", first produced in 1872. Interestingly this particular design was *"one of the more popular papers…used in one of the smaller rooms at St James's Palace"*[19]. The splendid interior photographs (Figs 42-45), probably taken by Gordon Locksley Salt in the spring of 1885, show that the Victorian taste for cluttered rooms crammed with exotic objects was greatly indulged at Milner Field. A large bay window gave a good view of the park, while also allowing light to flood the room. Local man, Trevor Meek, who visited the derelict house in 1941, vividly recalled this bay as being almost the size of a small room and likened its ceiling to *"looking up inside an umbrella"*[20], with ribs springing from a central boss.

Titus Jnr spared no expense in ensuring the house's fixtures and fittings were in keeping with the fabric of the building. The library's walls were lined with oak bookshelves while elsewhere teak, cedar, mahogany, walnut and chestnut panelling was used. In his library were works by Shakespeare, Dickens and Walter Scott, alongside many scientific and historical volumes and also a copy of the Koran.

His leather-bound collection, with many books displaying the family crest in gold tooling, would eventually find its way to the Old Rectory at Thorp Arch, Wetherby, where the family later lived and many of their belongings were auctioned off in December 1978. The marble fireplaces, which were such striking features in the principal rooms, appear to have met an ignoble end. Decidedly unfashionable after the Second World War, the Gothic overmantles were ripped-out and broken up during the demolition work. This was confirmed recently by a local lady whose garden boasts a piece of heavily-veined marble which her father salvaged from the site of the house.

Fig 50: Titus Jnr was a skilled wood and metal turner; he made the ivory bell pushes above, used throughout the house, on his own lathe in the workshop at Milner Field.

Titus Jnr was an accomplished turner of wood and ivory and built a workshop with a water-driven lathe at the house. He made and presented a number of ceremonial trowels and mallets in the nineteenth century and Denys Salt, his grandson, recalled recently with some amusement how his aunt had several of these silver trowels in her possession and chose to have them all melted down to make a silver tray which bears an inscription testifying to its earlier incarnation! (see Fig 80).

Fig 51: A collection of Titus Jnr's woodworking tools.

The ornamental ivory mason's mallet he fashioned for his young son to use in laying the foundation stone at Milner Field is still in the family's possession (see Fig 81). An interesting contemporary account of life at Milner Field can be gleaned from the diaries of nineteenth century physician Dr John Deakin Heaton. Heaton's journals were published posthumously and were edited by Sir Thomas Wemyss Reid, Editor of the Leeds Mercury.

Dr Heaton's diaries were very extensive; we are told they numbered "*seven or eight closely written quarto volumes, each of many hundreds of pages*" and are assured that they "*will be exceedingly valuable as a picture of domestic life in an English provincial town in the reign of Queen Victoria*".

Dr Heaton, who lived in Leeds and died in 1880, was a friend of Titus Jnr and moved in society circles within West Yorkshire. Heaton also recognised the worth of humbler citizens - from factory girls to Sunday school scholars - and they were often invited to spend time at his house or to enjoy his gardens.

On 2nd April, 1875 the Doctor's diary entry records a visit to the recently-built Milner Field. The account is given here in full:

"*In the afternoon, Fanny and I went to dine at Mr Salt's, of Milner Field, near Saltaire, and to stay the night there. The carriage met us at the Shipley station, and we drove through Saltaire, and then for about a mile through their own grounds to the house, Milner Field, a gorgeous mansion within, massive and imposing without, in the early style of domestic Gothic which is at this time favoured by what may be called the pre-Raphaelite School of Art. The name of the architect is Harris of London.*

Mrs Titus Salt is Edward Crossley's sister. She is a pretty, elegant woman having three children, the eldest about 11 years old the youngest a baby.

We entered a large hall, carpeted with thick Turkey carpets, which also cover the corridors and prevail generally. There is an immense, massive, stone structure forming the fireplace, and there is a large organ in a carved oak case. There is stained glass in the window illustrative of some history or legend, I think.

After being shown to our bedroom, the walls of which are wainscoted with oak, we sat in the Library until dinner-time. This room has an alabaster fireplace which forms a most prominent feature, carved, and rising in stories to the ceiling and decorated with tiles about the grate. There are oak bookcases, carved and further decorated with paintings on gilt grounds.

A Mister Miall, (brother of the Leeds curator) and his wife, and a Mr and Mrs Martin from Manchester, were other guests.

The Dining Room had some beautiful mural paintings over the fireplace, also on a gilt ground, by some eminent London artist.

Fig 52: The billiard room at Milner Field: it was here that Titus Jnr died.

After Dinner we sat in the Drawing Room which also has a large, alabaster chimney piece, rising to the height of the room, more elaborate than that in the Library. Numerous costly ornaments in china, carvings, etc., decorated the room.

During the evening Mr Salt took us to see his work room, where he has a very complete lathe worked by a water engine, which he can start at any minute; furnished with an elaborate set of eccentric and other chucks and a great variety of fine tools.

From there we were taken to the Billiard Room where the three gentlemen established themselves for a game with a supply of pipes and cigars. As this was not in my way, I came away with Fanny, and we retired to our bed in good time.

Saturday 3rd April; Fanny had her breakfast in bed. I breakfasted with the company about 9 o'clock, after which Fanny joined us and we went with Mr T. Salt to see his conservatories [here he is referring to the glasshouses]. These are at a considerable distance from the house so that rather more walking was required than quite suited Fanny.

The grounds at present are rather bare-looking, having no large trees. The conservatories are most extensive and complete, like everything else about the establishment.

We went through a succession of vineries, pine houses, stores, orchard houses, etc. Many gardeners were at work throughout.

When we returned, the carriage was at the door to take us to the station for our return to Leeds. We said good-bye and commenced our journey, and in due time we comfortably reached our small and simple-looking residence"[21].

Titus Jnr, with his keen interest in technology, was to pioneer some ground breaking experiments from Milner Field. The telephone, whilst still in its infancy, underwent amateur trials at the house.

In 1877, together with Professor W. F. Barratt from the British Association, Lord Houghton, Edward Crossley, Mr Gilpin (Superintendent of Telegraphs at Bradford) and an electrician

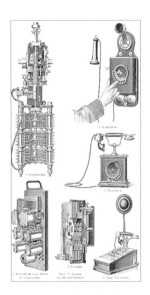

Fig 53: Early telephonic equipment. Titus Jnr would have used a system similar to this.

called Davis, he carried out some initial experiments within the offices of Salts Mill. Wires were laid through several offices and a telephone was attached to each end. A report in the *Shipley and Saltaire Times* declared that *"the distinctness and accuracy with which various questions and answers were interchanged by several members of the party, prompted them to further endeavours"[22].* The more eminent members of the party then retired to Milner Field taking a telephone with them, leaving at the mill the electrician and Mr Gilpin. The two buildings, a mile and three quarters distant, were linked by Titus Jnr's private telegraph wire and Mr Gilpin was then requested to read from the daily newspaper into the device. Lord Houghton listened and relayed the content to the rest of his party who, having consulted another copy of the same journal, pronounced it correct. *"Do you hear what we say?"* asked the men at the mill, *"Yes, go on"* was the response from the Salt group at the house. Mr Gilpin was then informed that a tune on the violin would be played by nine year old Master Harold Salt and it was apparently heard with great clarity. Mr Gilpin then requested that the boy play *"The Last Rose of Summer"* (causing the journalist to remark wryly that it was a *"somewhat unreasonable request ... as Summer itself is yet a stranger"*). This tune did not, however, appear to be in young Harold's repertoire, so the unfortunate Mr Gilpin was treated to a second rendition of the National Anthem! After dinner, the organ in the hallway at Milner Field was played into the device and, although Mr Davis could discern it was an instrument of some kind, its exact nature was impossible to ascertain. On the following day, a Saturday, the trials continued. A Miss Hanson, present in the offices at the mill, gave a performance of a verse of "*Kathleen Mavourneen*" to which Titus Jnr responded that he had heard every note and word distinctly. Three of those at Milner Field then sang "*The Canadian Boat Song*" and this was also heard perfectly at the mill. The two parties then took it in turns to recite alternating lines of a rhyme which, upon its successful conclusion, delighted Titus Jnr so much he cried "*Bravo! Bravo!*" into the mouthpiece. The Bell telephone used weighed about half a pound, was six inches long and could be carried in the pocket in its mahogany case. A female voice (that of Mrs Salt or Miss Hanson in this case) was transmitted with greater clarity due to its natural higher pitch. In our technologically-advanced age, it is

Fig 54: Telephone communication was established between
Milner Field and the mill offices, seen above.

interesting to read of the incredulity that greeted these experiments "*it is difficult to fully realise the fact that one is in actual verbal communication with some person miles away. It is such a 'still, small voice' that one hears – a voice true to its own peculiar character, but softened, and sweetened, and purified of its harsher sounds, like music borne on a summer breeze*"[23].

Two years later, further micro-telephonic experiments were carried out and technological advances enabled the service from Square Congregational Church, Halifax - given by the Reverend Dr Mellor - to be relayed to the house. The *Shipley and Saltaire Times* pronounced the experiment "*novel, instructive and interesting*"[24] and described the link up at some length. The Church was connected with Dean Clough (the Crossley's enterprise), forwarded by the Post Office to Midland Buildings, from there it was linked to the Salt warehouse at Well Street in Bradford, which in turn was linked to Milner Field via the offices of the Mill in Saltaire.

Fig 55: The Prince and Princess of Wales at the tree planting in the grounds of Milner Field, June 1882. Gordon Salt on the extreme right was at Winchester school during the ceremony and was later, rather cheekily, photographically patched into the print, the re-toucher even going to the length of utilising the leg of Lord Ponsonby, whom Gordon replaced.

High Life at Milner Field

The seal was set on Titus Jnr's position within county society when, between the 22nd and 24th of June 1882, he and his wife played host to Their Royal Highnesses The Prince and Princess of Wales - the future King Edward VII and Queen Alexandra. The royal couple were in the district to perform, among other duties, the opening of the Bradford Technical School (now College) on Great Horton Road.

The royal couple were entertained in lavish style, as the extensive menus in French bearing the Prince of Wales's feathers testify (see Fig 59). The Salt family's private archives contain much interesting correspondence relating to the

Fig 56: The inscribed tree planting spade, and the Prince's cigar, both seen in the image above. Today they form part of the Salt family archive.

*Fig 57 & 58: 2nd West Yorkshire Yeoman Cavalry in the
courtyard of Milner Field await the Royal couple.*

preparations for the royal visits and it is clear that Titus Jnr was determined to make a good impression, regardless of expense. A supplier from Sheffield itemised the new bed linen – from Saxony wool royal blankets to "*sheets specially designed and embroidered on the turn-over of the top sheet with a wreath encircling royal monograms surmounted by the plume, with the Order of the Garter below*" and a "*white toilet quilt specially designed and manufactured and trimmed with hand-wrought Italian point lace of first quality specially designed with emblems worked in each scallop*". Salt also commissioned a new scoreboard cabinet in the Gothic style for the billiard room from Marsh and Jones.

On the evening of Friday 23rd June, the three Webling sisters performed songs and recited poetry and prose before a hand-picked audience while, on the hilltops surrounding the estate, bonfires crackled to welcome the royal visitors. The Prince and Princess were escorted to and from the house by the 2nd West Yorkshire Yeoman Cavalry and photographs exist showing the cavalcade assembling in the courtyard (Figs 57-58). The Prince planted a tree in the grounds (Fig 55) to mark the visit and Denys Salt relates how his father, Harold, then a boy of 13, secretly retrieved the trademark cigar butt discarded by the future King. Wrapped in thick cartridge paper, this memento remains in the family's possession to this day! (Fig 56).

In an interesting sidenote, it appears that the popular actress Lillie Langtry was also in Bradford at the time of the visit. Langtry, of course, had been the Prince's 'official' mistress for some time and they had in fact built a lovenest together

*Fig 59: Menu from the
first Royal Visit of 1882.*

45

Fig 60: The rather bizarre sight of the Prince of Wales, with the Princess by his side, raising his hat to his mistress, Mrs Langtry, on their departure from Bradford.

in Bournemouth in 1877. Princess Alexandra knew of her husband's infidelity, but as duty and social mores of the time dictated, she turned a blind eye to his diversions.

It has long been thought that the organisers of social events to which the Prince was invited were also discreetly advised to ensure an invitation was also extended to Mrs Langtry, otherwise the Prince would be likely to decline. Corroboration of this suggestion appears in the collected correspondence between the Palace and the Salts. In a letter from Lord Ponsonby at Marlborough House, unusually marked *"private"* and dated 22nd May 1882, it is suggested in response to Titus Jnr's question that *"Mrs Langtry might be asked after dinner on one of the nights"* (original emphasis). Mrs Langtry's presence was also noted by the *Illustrated London News* on 1st July 1882, which featured an engraving of Their Royal Highnesses waving to Mrs Langtry during their Bradford visit. (Fig 60).

Fig 61: The second royal tree planting in the grounds of Milner Field, May 1887. Princess Beatrice and her husband, centre, are flanked by an ill looking Titus Jnr and Catherine Salt (blurred as a result of moving).

Fig 62: Princess Beatrice of Battenberg
and her husband Henry.

Titus Jnr's devotion to his work continued unabated and, despite having been diagnosed with a heart condition in 1885, he threw himself into preparations for the Royal Yorkshire Jubilee Exhibition, intended to raise sufficient funds to defray the £12,000 cost of the Saltaire Science and Art Schools built in 1886 in memory of his late father. The twelve-acre exhibition site in Saltaire even included a complete Japanese village and was opened by the Queen's daughter, Princess Beatrice of Battenberg, and her husband Henry on 6th May 1887.

Like the previous royal couple, they too stayed at Milner Field. The house must have made a magnificent impression as the royal visitors' carriage made its way up the drive, eventually reaching the Gothic arch. As the *Shipley Times* reported, "*At the entrance to the courtyard was an arch covered with ivy, which bore a circular inscription in plush, with a white background, welcoming the royal guests to Milner Field. Over the portal was the presentment of the crown in flowers, with purple cinerarias to represent the jewels. The conservatory was lighted with small coloured incandescent lamps, concealed among the foliage and had a lovely effect. The dinner party included many of the distinguished guests who headed the procession*"[25].

The Prince and Princess were afforded every courtesy there even, as an intriguingly informal letter from the Princess's Lady-in-Waiting Lady Cavendish records, a separate bed in their adjoining dressing room "*in case they have foreign sleeping ideas!*"

Fig 63: This splendid previously unpublished photograph of Titus Jnr was taken in New York. He made several trips to the U.S. attending to the Salt family business interests which had been established there.

47

Fig 64: Construction under way for the
Saltaire Royal Yorkshire Jubilee Exhibition.

Mrs Salt was naturally eager that a good impression was created and Lady Cavendish was spurred on to offer further guidance. Describing the Princess as "*not clever, but intelligent*", she helpfully added "*no doubt at this moment babies would be an uppermost topic! - they (the Royal family, not the babies!) are all affectionate and forthcoming and domestic*". Ominously, it is possible that the strain the exhibition was taking on Titus Jnr was already beginning to show, as the writer concluded by hoping that "*Mr Salt is better than when I was with you*". This visit was also commemorated with a tree planting within the grounds (See Fig 61). Interestingly, local people recall the royal commemorative trees and their plaques but no trace of them can now be found.

Fig 65: This photograph of the fully working locomotive "Beatrice"
(named after the royal visitor), gives some idea of the scale and complexity of the exhibition.

The Jubilee Exhibition though was not a success and Titus Jnr's total deficit stood at a shade under £8,450. His friends and family were quick to note the toll this exhausting enterprise had taken on him, though their pleas for him to reduce his workload characteristically went unheeded.

Family Tragedy

On Saturday 19th November 1887, Titus Jnr paid one of his usual visits to Saltaire, calling in at the Institute and the Art & Science Schools before walking down Victoria Road puffing on a cigar. To those who saw him that

Fig 66: Royal Doulton stand in one of the specially-constructed exhibition halls.

day, he appeared in good health and there was no apparent cause for concern. Later, feeling slightly indisposed, he lunched quietly back at the house after which he took a short walk in the grounds before retiring to the billiard room at around 3pm to rest. Shortly afterwards he was discovered unconscious by his wife and an urgent telephone call was placed to the family's physician, Dr Ellis, who at the time was attending a meeting of the Governors of the Salts Schools in the Institute.

His arrival came too late and Titus Jnr was pronounced dead: he was forty-four years of age. The local shock and grief were widespread and the company was dealt a heavy blow by his death.

The funeral cortège assembled at Milner Field at 11am on Wednesday 23rd November where the pall-bearing party – made up of servants and gardeners from the house, the cashier and foreman of long-standing from the mills, the Secretary of the Salt Schools, the Head of the Central Schools and an old servant of Sir Titus' – transferred the oak coffin to the hearse.

Police officers from across the district lined the carriage drive as the forty carriages passed solemnly by on their way to the church at Saltaire where Titus Jnr was interred next to his father in the family mausoleum.

Figs 67 & 68: Titus Jnr was laid to rest next to his father in the Salt family mausoleum (Left: exterior, right : interior) adjacent to the church on Victoria Road, Saltaire. The tomb would eventually contain the remains of seven members of the Salt family.

Titus Jnr's drive and commitment to work were the making of the man and a significant factor in his early demise. An un-named close friend, who wrote an appreciation of him for the *Bradford Observer* recalled "*He had no mercy on himself. He spent himself without stint for the objects he took up. He seemed incapable of being quiet or of taking rest. He did not care for sport and other diversion [and] did not shoot or fish or hunt. It would have been better for him if he had. He did, however, delight in his gardens, and his extensive glass houses at Milner Field were admirably designed and managed, all by himself...He was never really happy unless he was at work and he always worked hard....Some time ago, when I was pressing on him the need of rest, and care, and quiet, he said: "Why should I rest or be careful of myself? I don't want to live a long life; but as long as I do live, I will work and I will enjoy myself*"[26].

Shortly before Christmas 1888, the widowed Catherine Salt turned to her brother Henry Crossley for financial help and the house and estate were mortgaged to him. Mrs Salt and her four children Gordon, Harold, Lawrence and Isabel continued to live at Milner Field but played a somewhat diminished role in the locality.

Edward Salt of Ferniehurst was now the only family member with a seat on the board, but times were changing and the market for Salt's renowned lustrous cloth – spun by blending alpaca weft with cotton or silk warps - was collapsing as women's fashions embraced softer, more easily draped materials. Attempts were made to diversify, but the company's degree of specialisation made this difficult and the United States McKinley trade tariffs of 1890 and unsuccessful expansion plans further added to the company's woes.

On 3rd September 1892, the firm of Sir Titus Salt Bart. Sons & Co. Ltd went into liquidation. Both Edward Salt and Charles Stead (of The Knoll), who had used their houses as collateral, lost their homes when the Bradford Banking Company foreclosed on their loans. In June 1893 the company was sold to a four-man syndicate from Bradford – coal magnate John Rhodes and woolmen John Maddocks, Isaac Smith and James Roberts. Roberts and his family moved into the Mill Manager's house, known as The Knoll, recently vacated by Stead.

Despite turbulent times in the commercial world, Milner Field could still be a splendid backdrop to a magnificent event and one such instance was a fancy dress ball the widowed Mrs Salt was to host at the house on 9th October 1895 to "bring out" her daughter Isabel, who was then nineteen. Mrs Salt penned a press account of the ball which was printed in *The Gentlewoman* on 26th October:

"A most successful fancy dress ball took place on Wednesday, 9th inst. at Milner Field, the well known residence of Mrs Titus Salt.

The quaint style of the mansion lent itself to the occasion, as that of a merely conventional house would have failed to do. With instinctive good taste, the decorations were of the simplest, thus permitting the brown oak panelling to fulfil its natural purpose as an effective background for the many rich and uncommon colours and fashions worn by the company.

Fig 69: A serene Catherine Salt in later life.

The electric light was carried to the outside of the beautiful stained glass windows in the hall, the effect being of clear day-light streaming through. The supper tables, nine on each side of the upper corridor, were elegantly arranged beneath arches of ivy, each arch bearing an electric light. The winter garden was beautified by choice Japanese lanterns forming a picturesque retreat for the gaily dressed crowd. All the lighting throughout the house was under the direction of Mr Gordon Salt and Mr Lawrence Salt who are enthusiastic electrical engineers.

Dancing went on in the dining room and drawing room – Johnstons well known band from Manchester being stationed in an alcove between the two rooms.

Amongst many superb costumes one can only select a few which appeared particularly elegant. Mrs Titus Salt, the hostess, looked charming in a carefully studied historical dress, as Queen Mary Stuart. Her young daughter as Olivia Primrose wore a white flowered brocade over a lilac petticoat with a large black picture hat with white feather. Mrs Crossley (Grandmother dear) – a living illustration of Mrs Molesworth's well known story, even to the walking stick. Miss Crossley (Queen Henrietta Maria) in an elegant 17th Century dress, with hair arranged in short ringlets. Miss Fison – a Cairene woman, veiled, with only the eyes visible, Eastern fashion. Miss Cunningham as Madame la Marquise. Miss Ferrand in rich Watteau brocade with hair dressed high and powdered as Poudrée Watteau. Mrs Stanhope in white satin, first Empire style copied from a family miniature of Lady Hamilton. Mrs Yorke in a bright effective dress as an operetta Queen. Miss Rome in a genuine old family dress of 1750 date, one of those stiff brocades described by my own grandmother. Miss Kitson (Incroyable) in a fantastic coat and skirt with three cornered hat of the Directoire period, most becoming to her. Miss Sybil Cunningham (Blue China) a pretty blue brocade with blue pattern and blue sash, Gainsborough hat, poudrée. Miss Locking as a witch with signs of the Zodiac in black velvet, black sugar loaf hat and broom stick.

Amongst the men we must notice Mr Harold Salt as Faust, in peacock blue striped with pale blue, Mr Gordon Salt and Mr Lawrence Salt as Courtiers, Louis XVI time. Later in the evening Mr Lawrence Salt became a Cairo merchant.

Sir Malby Crofton, Deputy Lieutenant, and Mr Maxwell Rouse were in Highland uniform, Mr Fison in Admiral's uniform. Judge Gales in Levee dress. Mr Marchetti as Claude Duval, with fawn coloured redingote with green tippet, three cornered hat – most effective. Mr Whitwell and Mr H Wade in Egyptian dress, full white trousers to the knee, richly embroidered jacket, fez or silk turban. Mr Whitwell as Pickwick, an excellent living picture *of Dickens' immortal hero. Mr G Osborne as Jack Point, the jester in the Yeoman of the Guard fur coat, red velvet breeches with small bells, a jester's cap and hood and bauble. Mr C Scott (Charles Surface) in plum coloured coat, flowered waistcoat, knee breeches, poudré. Mr A Gates as Beau Brummel, claret coloured suit, lace tie and ruffles. Mr W Briggs in Hugenot dress, black velvet coat, yellow stockings – a good presentation of the figure in Millais' picture.*

Dancing was kept up with great spirit till 3 o'clock."

A delightful photograph exists of party-goers seated in the conservatory with a woman dressed as Grace Darling seated with the group (Fig 70).

Clouds had begun to gather on the horizon and the carefree days for the Salts at Milner Field were drawing to a close.

Fig 70: Young members of the Salt family, including Harold, pose in fancy dress.
Popular Victorian heroine Grace Darling is depicted on the right.

The Roberts' Years

By 1902, James Roberts had bought out his business partners and took on the role as Managing Director of Salts *"as Napoleon shed his consuls, so he shed the rest of his syndicate"*, wrote Roberts' granddaughter Sybil in her autobiography[27]. Contemporary newspaper reports, however, do not paint Roberts' emergence as sole owner in quite so ruthless or dramatic terms.

Roberts applied himself with characteristic zeal to turning around the fortunes of Salts. He modernised working practices in every department and ploughed money into the failing enterprise, purchasing new plant and equipment. He introduced a raft of economies and secured new customers in eastern Europe (he was later to present £10,000 to the University of Leeds for the foundation and maintenance of a Chair of Russian Language and Literature) replacing those lost in America. Roberts had considerable experience of trading with eastern Europe dating back to the 1870s and early 1880s, even learning the Russian language to more finely hone his skills.

In 1903 Roberts, now well-established, bought Milner Field and the estate from Titus Jnr's widow, who was removing to Denton Park, Ilkley, and moved there from The Knoll with wife Elizabeth and his family. Elizabeth Roberts (née Foster) was of yeoman stock and her father had been a tenant-farmer at Brass Castle, a farm at Harden on the Ferrand Estate. They were now certainly moving up in the world. The contract of sale, dated 17th January 1903, set the purchase price at £26,000.

Appended to the contract is an interesting schedule of sentimental artefacts scheduled for removal before the sale which Mrs Salt had drawn up and upon which both parties had agreed. It reads:

"An organ at present in the Front Hall; Circular Coat of Arms in glass over the doorway; Cushions in the circular window of the drawing room; Stained glass window over the outer door in the Round Hall; Detachable window-seat in Library; Leather pictures attached to the fitments in the book-case at the opposite end to the Library fire-place; Three panels and a frieze over the fire-place in the dining room, which have already been removed; The dog stoves in the Billiard Room and Hall; All Ivory portion of door handles and bell pushes; Two Tapestries hanging in Staircase Hall; Cue racks and marking board in Billiard Room"[28].

Though some sundry items from the billiard room were earmarked for removal by Mrs Salt, the hefty billiard table itself would presumably have been surplus to her requirements.

At some stage later in the house's life though the table was removed and for a long time it stood in Hopewell House, Lightcliffe, Halifax where it enjoyed many more years' service. Fittingly, a photograph of it *in situ* at Milner Field hung on the wall nearby. Recent enquiries by the authors have revealed that the table has since been removed once again – in itself a task of some logistical complexity – and its whereabouts are now unknown. One can only hope that it is still in regular use and that its history is not lost on its present owner. If the current owner should happen to read this book, perhaps he or she would be good enough to contact the publishers as a modern photograph would make a handsome addition to our photographic record.

The Roberts family moved into Milner Field on 1st June 1903, having first laid down their own special condition stipulating they should be given access to the property before Mrs Salt left, for purposes of *"putting into some part of the stables or coachhouses a new gas engine, dynamo and accumulators and to lay mains"*.

Fig 71: Sir James Roberts.

It was in this same year that Roberts would generously mark the one hundredth anniversary of the birth of the late Sir Titus Salt (and the fiftieth anniversary of the opening of the mills) by donating a bronze statue of Salt which can still be seen in Roberts Park to this day.

Sybil Bolton, recalled the Roberts' new family home in her autobiography:
"Not one twig broke the neatly rounded contour of the hawthorn hedge on either side of the mile long drive. Not one weed marred the vast expanse of gravel in the great courtyard in front of the house. And the pots of musk of Brass Castle days had now reached the height of their efflorescence in an enormous winter garden where life-size statuary of Greek and Roman gods and goddesses, set on marble pedestals, nestled coyly or flaunted their physical perfection flamboyantly beneath spreading palms or other tropical verdure. There was a Louis Quinze drawing-room, all gold and green, with a grand piano to match. There was a Heppelwhite dining-room, with scarlet leather seats to the chairs. There was a vast library, preceded by an ante-room which was like nothing so much as the interior of the Albert Memorial would have been like if the Albert Memorial had had a furnished interior. The library itself was all velvet with bobbly tassels, and in the cupboards beneath the

bookshelves my grandmother kept boxes of sweets and biscuits, and, of course, her knitting, for the steel needles still clicked.

Mullioned, casemented windows looked out on smooth expanses of velvety lawns, grey balustrading, and cypress-dark topiary. There was, indeed, nothing radical about Milner Field. The cows and the hens on the home farm had pedigrees. The dogs were all gun dogs. The lake was stocked with trout.

It was Victorian Gothic, however, and progress had its place. Besides the Queen's bathroom [sic], where royalty had washed its hands after planting a tree in the garden, there was a pianola in the library. There was not only a huge organ in the hall, there was a telephone too. And the coachman who had taught my mother to drive a pair of spirited horses down the main street of Bradford had given way to a younger man who had discarded his tall coachman's hat, while retaining his breeches and leggings, in order to drive something which was called "the motor" [29].

Roberts and his family were to occupy Milner Field until about 1918 and furnished it in a markedly different style to the Salts. The Roberts' flamboyant taste, with rococo giltwood furniture echoing the ostentation of the French court, is vividly captured in a magnificent pair of photographs taken by Bedford Lemere (Figs 97 and 98). Harry Bedford Lemere specialised in architectural photographs but with an emphasis on decorative schemes. Working to commission – usually, but not always, from a householder – he used a 12 x 10 inch mahogany and brass stand camera with glass plates to capture a room and its décor to best effect. In this particular case it was Marsh and Jones of Leeds who commissioned the photographs of the Milner Field interiors, which were taken in July 1904. Marsh & Jones were very much 'general merchants' and would provide furniture in any style the householder desired. It is coincidental that they should have designed and made both Salt's 'reformed Gothic' and the Roberts' 'French rococo' furnishings. According to Roberts family descendents, it would appear that it was Elizabeth Roberts who had a taste for the flamboyant. Their later home in Perthshire was furnished in a more traditional style though it was she who was responsible for having the backgrounds to a pair of lifesize portraits of herself and her husband, which dated from 1903 and almost certainly hung at Milner Field, repainted in a more ostentatious fashion in 1927. They now hang in the dining room at Strathallen.

Family gatherings at Christmastime must have been splendid affairs. Sybil Bolton remembered *"the Christmas tree at Milner Field was in the Winter Garden. When you got bored with the bright lights on the tree, you could wander round among the palm trees* and stare up at the sightless eyes of the Greek and Roman gods and goddesses, and lay a hot little hand on the cold perfection of their marble feet, and so catch, for a moment, the chilly remoteness of Olympus… In due course my grandfather [Roberts] would come in dressed up as Father Christmas, and if you were sufficiently daring to cry out "But you're not Father Christmas – you're Grandpa!" you would get a look which somehow reminded you of the chilly remoteness of Olympus, and you would be more sure than ever that it was Grandpa and not Father Christmas"[30]. Bolton also described her childhood taunting of the family butler, Green, who would be working behind the iron bars which protected the silver in the butler's pantry. On one occasion, after much persuasion, he opened the huge safe for her and she was allowed to sit and gaze at a golden casket – which bore an image of the mill in relief and contained a scroll praising Roberts - which the millworkers had presented to her grandfather. When she suddenly rushed up and tried, with childish glee, to close the door of the safe trapping Green inside, he had shaken with fright at the thought of being suffocated inside.

Fig 72: The gargantuan task of running the enormous
mill at Saltaire took a heavy toll on James Roberts.

Elizabeth Roberts' elderly mother, Bella Foster, also lived with the family at Milner Field, though it appeared that the old lady – who was by this time in her nineties – occupied the nursery rooms. She lived alongside much banished Victorian furniture which had been moved upstairs to make way for the Louis XV and Heppelwhite pieces in the principal rooms.

Fig 73: Roberts Park. The park is the only reminder of Roberts' tenure at Salts.

The ageing Mrs Foster was visited in the nursery by her great grandchildren whom she would try to encourage to sing hymns to her, with little result, in exchange for a half-crown. The old lady died in 1912.

James Roberts was greatly involved in the public life of the locality, serving on the Urban District Council of Shipley from 1897 and as its Chairman from 1904. As well as managing the gargantuan enterprise at Salts, he was also involved with the West Riding County Council, was Chairman of the Rivers Board, a Justice of the Peace and became joint owner of the Yorkshire Observer. Roberts followed in Salt's philanthropic footsteps once he had secured his business empire; he supported the Bingley Cottage Hospital, gave Hirst Wood to the people of Shipley and paid for Dr Barnardo's *"Roberts House"* in Harrogate. But despite his popularity and successful career, Roberts suffered personal tragedies which coloured both his reputation and that of Milner Field.

His eldest son, James William (known in the family as Willie), had died on 3rd June 1898 at The Knoll, aged twenty-four. For health reasons he had lived for some years in South Africa. While there he suffered another bout of ill health and this hastened his return to Britain. On his homecoming bad weather had brought on pneumonia and within a month of his arrival at The Knoll he died.

In 1904, a year after moving into Milner Field, James Roberts' youngest son, eleven-year-old Jack, drowned while fishing from a rock at Portrush, Ireland during a family holiday. A newspaper account of the time details an attempted rescue of the boy by a fellow fisherman.

Roberts was left with only two sons - Bertram Foster who worked with him as joint Managing Director and the younger Harry who was a departmental head. Roberts was created a Baronet in 1909 in King Edward VII's Birthday Honours. Barely two years later his gifted son Bertram developed neuritis (an inflamation of the nervous system) and died, on 11th January 1912, following a seven week illness. He was thirty-six.

Bill Tegner, grandson of Bertram Foster Roberts, told us that his mother's family was moving *"from Nonconformism to Anglicanism (for social reasons, one imagines), so the christening of Bertram Foster Roberts's four children was put off until 1918. At the christening, the vicar mentioned the sad death of the children's father, which caused tears and consternation, since they had never been informed of this. They had simply been told that he had "gone away"*[31].

Roberts provided an impressive grave in Shipley's Nab Wood cemetery for his son. Some years later the grave would be desecrated when thieves hacked through the pillars supporting an ornate bronze canopy on the tomb and stole it.

Of his four sons, only Harry now remained and the war clouds that would soon engulf Europe had begun to gather.

By the autumn of 1915, in response to a nationwide feeling that there were many 'slackers' who had refused to volunteer for service, voluntary recruitment for the armed forces was ended by Lord Derby, the newly-appointed Secretary of State for War. Instead he introduced a registration scheme, which was to bear his name, in which all unmarried men between the ages of eighteen and forty-one were to register and await call-up papers.

The spinning and manufacturing of cloth was considered an essential industry and at Salt's the Great War had brought with it some large contracts for khaki uniform material. The company were also busily obtaining orders in Russia and South America, where they had strong connections, and which complied with the government's policy of maintaining the fullest export trade. By March 1916,

Fig 74: Alice Roberts would be embroiled in a national scandal.

59

the company had released more than thirty-three percent of its workforce eligible to serve and problems were mounting as essential staff dwindled.

Harry Roberts had been keen to play his part and had wanted to enlist in 1915. Although his father had told him that he would not be fit to bear the name of an Englishman if he had not wanted to serve, he eventually managed to persuade him that the running of the company would be very severely affected by his leaving. Bowing to the pressure, Harry reluctantly attested as the holder of a reserved occupation under the Derby Scheme, in order to remain as Managing Director and Manager of the Wool, Dress Goods and Linings departments.

Apparently, despite assurances given to Sir James Roberts that Harry would not be made to serve, the District Tribunal refused to be swayed and Roberts' pleas fell on deaf ears. Their insistence that Harry serve was an enormous blow to Roberts and on 4th March 1916, the *Daily News* carried the dramatic headline "Saltaire Mills to close – if certain men are taken – decision of Sir James Roberts".

In a letter to the Tribunal, Sir James Roberts put his case stating *"the necessity of closing down at Saltaire I contemplate with horror. The loss would be enormous to me and others, and I need hardly say that physical limitations are the only ones that could cause this step to be taken. What I wish to do is to clear myself of responsibility for the taking of such a step"*.

Harry Roberts appealed against his call-up order, and his father appeared personally before the Appeal tribunal at the end of March. In his statement he refuted allegations made in local newspapers that he had threatened to close the Mills if his son was not relieved from military service, but highlighted the disastrous consequences Harry's leaving would bring about - it would be "impossible", he said, for him to go on. His arguing, though, was to no avail and the appeal was rejected. Harry presented himself at the Keighley Recruiting Headquarters at the end of March and was given fourteen days leave of absence in which to arrange his affairs.

The forebodings were sadly fulfilled when Second Lieutenant Harry Roberts, serving with his regiment the Royal Dublin Fusiliers, was seriously wounded fighting at the front in France in September 1917. No longer fit to work, he retired to Jersey. Sir James Roberts' woes were added to when his extensive business dealings in Russia suffered as the Bolsheviks seized control of the country in 1917. Without sons to share his workload and with a reduced workforce, the sole managerial responsibility bore heavily on the shoulders of the ageing Roberts.

Tired and ailing, in 1918 he was finally forced to relinquish control, retiring to Strathallan Castle at Machany in Perthshire, the seat of the Earls of Perth, which he had bought along with its 6,000 acre estate, in 1910. The business was sold for £2,000,000 to a consortium made up of Sir James Hill, Sir Henry Whitehead, Arthur Hill and Ernest Gates. On Roberts' departure from Saltaire, his gifts to his employees were estimated at £25,000: a considerable sum at that time.

Sir James Roberts would later look back on the circumstances of Harry's call-up with barely-concealed bitterness. From Strathallan, Roberts had been in correspondence with Saltaire Cricket Club in connection with the running costs of, and access to, Saltaire Park which he appears to have still been funding and from which, incidentally, he insisted no member of the public should be excluded.

In a private letter dated 17th December 1918 to Mr Fred Atkinson of the Cricket Club, Roberts expanded on the injustice he felt he had suffered at the Mill during the war. *"After the Military Service Act came into force"* he wrote, *"the Advisory Committee – knowing the conditions – decided to advise that my son Harry should not be called up. The Military Representative, Mr J. A. Burton, whose business it was to provide men for the army, said he could not ask for him. Notwithstanding, the Local Tribunal decided that he must go. This, I am told, is the only instance on record in which a Local Tribunal has acted in direct opposition both to the Advisory Committee and the Military Representative. I was left alone at Saltaire Mills, with the result that in attempting the impossible I seriously broke down."*

In a further private letter in February 1919, Roberts' secretary revealed *"Sir James has the opinion, rightly or wrongly, that it was the deliberate intention of the District Council and of the Military Tribunal (four out of five of whose members, I understand, are Vice Presidents of the [Cricket] Club) to drive him out of the district"*.

For Roberts though, any hope though that his family's run of misfortune had come to an end was premature. Roberts' second daughter Alice had, in around 1903, married Norman Cecil Rutherford, elder son of Shipley doctor John James Rutherford, against her parents' wishes. It was this marriage which would heap more heartache upon the Roberts family and make them the focus of a national scandal to boot.

At 10.20 on the evening of 13th January 1919, Sir James' son-in-law, now Lieutenant-Colonel Rutherford, knocked on the door of 13 Clarendon Road in London's fashionable Notting Hill district. He asked to speak with a Major Miles Seton who was at the house visiting his cousin. On learning of the visitor, Major Seton left the drawing room and ushered Rutherford into the dining room where the two men spoke for about a quarter of an hour before Rutherford drew his revolver and shot the forty-four year old Major three times in the chest at close quarters. It transpired that Major Seton, who had served with the Australian Medical Corps, was having an affair with Alice Rutherford.

At the trial Rutherford pleaded insanity and it is said that he spent a number of years in a mental institution, though Julia Bolton Holloway, great granddaughter of Sir James Roberts, suggests that he served his sentence in Broadmoor and was a model prisoner there. Roberts' relationship with his daughter seemingly never fully recovered. They were never to be close again, though she did appear in a group photograph at Strathallen to mark her parents' diamond wedding anniversary. In 1927 she changed her name back to Roberts by Deed Poll and her father helped with her legal costs.

In 1924, Sir James and Lady Roberts eventually settled at The Hall in Fairlight, Hastings, a huge, castellated mansion. Lady Elizabeth Roberts died in July 1935 and Sir James – as if unwilling to see in the new year without his beloved wife – died on old year's night, 1935. They both lie buried in the churchyard there, alongside Kathleen, Alice's second daughter.

Attempts were made to sell Milner Field and its sprawling estate in 1922 and a lavish catalogue was produced; but being so rambling, unfashionable and costly to run and repair it remained unsold.

Fig 75: Sir James and Lady Roberts at Fairlight Hall.

The Gates Family

Ernest Gates, a Londoner who had become associated with the wool trade as the London salesman for a West Bowling firm, had come to Bradford in his twenties and established Ernest Henry Gates & Co. around 1909, later taking over Providence Mills from Isaac Sowden & Sons. Following the syndicate's purchase of Salts, Sir Henry Whitehead became Chairman of the Directors and Gates was made Managing Director, moving from "Kirkfield" in Baildon to Milner Field in the summer of 1923 along with his wife, Eva. The couple had one son, Ernest Everard Gates.

Gates' wife had been ill for many years and suffered from what the *Yorkshire Evening Argus* called "*an obscure disease*"[32]. She was confined to a wheelchair and it is said that she liked to sit in the conservatory conversing with the stable boys whom she would ask to place small bets on her behalf. Intriguingly, a photograph has recently come to light which shows Mrs Gates – and even possibly her husband, – at a gathering in Milner Field's conservatory. This very rare photograph is reproduced below (Fig 77) and is owned by Baildon resident, Mrs Billie Smith. It shows the annual staff party at Milner Field in 1923. Three year old Billie actually appears in the photograph (slightly obscured, to the right of the picture, with a rib-

Fig 76: Mr Ernest H. Gates

bon in her hair), with her grandmother (to the left of the table in an apron, standing) and her grandfather, Albert Bond, Head Gardener (at the back of the picture). Mrs Gates can be seen in the foreground in her wheelchair and to her right is her nursemaid (holding a party mask to her face) who provided twenty four hour care to the ailing mistress of the house. Two unnamed housemaids are seated at the end of the table. It is likely that the young man standing close to Mrs Gates is her

Fig 77: Annual staff party at Milner Field in 1923, also showing the solid west end wall of the conservatory in the background.

son, Everard. It is quite possible that the man seated at the head of the table (middle, background) is Ernest Gates himself. Billie's grandfather Albert Bond came from Coney Weston in Suffolk and worked as a gardener in Bradford for a Mr Smith who lived in what is now the Nurses' Home at the Bradford Royal Infirmary. He moved on to The Borrins in Baildon, which it is believed Mr Smith bought. He later became employed by Ernest Gates at Milner Field and his varied duties included raising and keeping pheasants for shooting parties at the house and working with the exotic fruits. He had more conventional skills, too, and regularly judged the chrysanthemum section at the Paxton horticultural show. In an odd twist of fate, Albert later went on to work for Lady Whitehead in Baildon and while in her employ fell through a rotting floor in a potting shed, developing gangrene in his foot and leg. In a fate that mirrored that of Gates himself, Bond died from his injuries at the age of fifty and is buried in Charlestown cemetery, Baildon.

Gates was an attentive and devoted husband whose care for his sick wife was exemplary but on 29th October 1923, within weeks of their arrival at Milner Field, Eva Gates died. In his wife's memory, Gates donated £33,000 to the Cambridge Research Centre with the purpose of completing the endowment of a School of Pathology for Cambridge University.

Despite his grief, Gates was successful at Salts but on 1st April 1925, less than eighteen months after the death of his wife, he died of septicaemia, aged fifty-one. The locals were shocked and many rumours as to the cause of his death soon circulated. The more inventive had him treading on a rusty nail protruding from the staircase in the house, while others cited a rose bush or barbed wire in the grounds or, more sportingly, an unlucky blow from a golf club. The stories soon became folklore, no doubt embellished with every re-telling as is often the case in tight-knit communities. All the gossip shared in common the dark and brooding mansion. The truth was rather less dramatic. Gates had, according to the *Yorkshire Observer*, suffered a "*slight and simple accidental injury*" to his foot, following a collision with what is only described as "*some obstruction*"[33] when out walking in the grounds of his other estate at Old Buckenham Hall in Norfolk. Gates was driven back to Milner Field for medical attention and attended by Mr Basil Hall and Dr Beetham. The abrasion to his foot caused him considerable pain and by Thursday 26th March concern had grown to the extent that Gates was removed to Mr Hall's nursing home at Eldon Place, Bradford. Following an operation to arrest the poisoning on 28th March, it was felt that his chances were now much improved and that the danger had been averted in time. A specialist from London was called in and he gave the opinion that the poison had not spread above Gates' knee. He continued to show signs of improvement but when the King's physician, Lord Dawson of Penn, examined him he expressed a grave opinion of his condition. Gates' decline was rapid and he was soon critically ill, dying shortly after noon on 1st April. Mourning was widespread and Gates' funeral cortège left Milner Field early on Saturday 4th April 1925 heading for Bradford Cathedral where the service took place.

The procession of forty motor carriages then made its way to Nab Wood cemetery where he was interred alongside his wife. Gates was certainly a wealthy man – his estate was to be calculated at £1m, with death duties of £400,000 – but like Salt and Roberts before him, he was a generous benefactor to many charitable causes and was held in great respect by the

Fig 78: The grave of Ernest Gates in Nab Wood cemetery.

people of Saltaire. It is rumoured that Gates' son moved to London and backed a play called *The White Bird*, which flopped badly. It is thought that he then emigrated to America. For those interested in researching more on the son of Ernest Gates, we came across a reference to an Ernest Everard Gates, born on 29th May 1903, as MP for the Middleton & Prestwich constituency in Lancashire on 22nd May 1940. The record shows his date of death as 12th October 1984 at the age of eighty one[34].

Death and ill-luck seemed to be dogging the occupants of Milner Field and yet more was to follow.

The Hollins Family

Arthur Remington Hollins, successor to Gates at Salts, was the house's final occupant, moving there with his wife Anne Neilson Hollins and sons Henry Edmund Hollins (known as Ted or Teddy) aged eighteen and Richard John Drennan Hollins (known as Dick) aged fourteen, in 1925.

Arthur Hollins, who was born in 1878, was formerly the Chairman and Managing Director of Messrs William Hollins & Company of Pleasley Vale, Nottinghamshire and, as the *Mansfield Reporter* perceptively put it "*a local loss will be Bradford's gain ... [Salts] have made an excellent choice*"[35]. The family were joined in the sprawling house by

Fig 79: This splendid triptych by Frederick Weekes gives some idea of the fine quality panels which he also painted for Milner Field, and whose whereabouts are unknown.
(Courtesy: Sim Fine Art, photograph by Matthew Hollow)

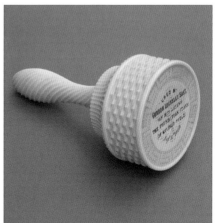

Fig 80: Left: Denys Salt and his late wife Eva holding the silver tray made from presentation trowels.

Fig 81: Right: Ceremonial ivory mason's mallet, made by Titus Jnr and used by his infant son Gordon to lay Milner Field's foundation stone on 11th September 1869.

Figs 82: Above & 83: Below. The orangery: then and now (2009).

*Examples of the Marsh &
Jones furniture originally
commissioned by Titus Jnr.*

*Much of this furniture is
now housed at Lotherton
Hall, nr Leeds.*

*Fig 84: Above.
The bedroom suite
along with much of the
remaining Salt furniture
is in excellent condition.*

*Fig 85: Above.
Charles Bevan's
magnificent Gothic
revival piano which once
graced Milner Field*

*Fig 86: Left.
A bedroom
washstand suite.*

Present day images of the cellars at Milner Field.

Fig 87: Left. Arched cellar entrance.

Fig 88: Below. Internal view of cellar entrance. This extensive complex of underground rooms lies underneath almost the entire site of the mansion.

Fig 89: Below. Rare image taken probably in the late 1950s or early 1960s from inside the hall, looking out to the courtyard. Dressed stone has been stripped away and the porch has almost completely disappeared.

Dresses made for Catherine Salt.

Fig 90: Right. The Mary Queen of Scots dress made for the fancy dress ball of 1895.

Fig 91: Below. Catherine Salt's pearl gown made by Alice Mason, Modes and Robes, 4 New Burlington Street, probably for the evening of the 1882 royal visit.

Fig 92: Below right. Pearl gown detail.

Fig 93: This photograph taken in 2005 shows some traces of the steps up to old Milner Field, which Titus Jnr incorporated into his new gardens. The old house's gateposts lay collapsed in the thick undergrowth and the lawn is long gone.

Fig 94: The distinctive carved pieces of masonry in the centre of this image come from the upper section of the drawing room bay window.
The inset shows the masonry in its original location.

Fig 95: The south face of Milner Field, c1885.

Fig 96: This very rare colour photograph from the late 1950s shows the house as a gaunt, roofless ruin: a sad reflection of its former glory.

Fig 97: Harry Bedford Lemere photograph of the drawing room, richly decorated in gold and green. July 1904.

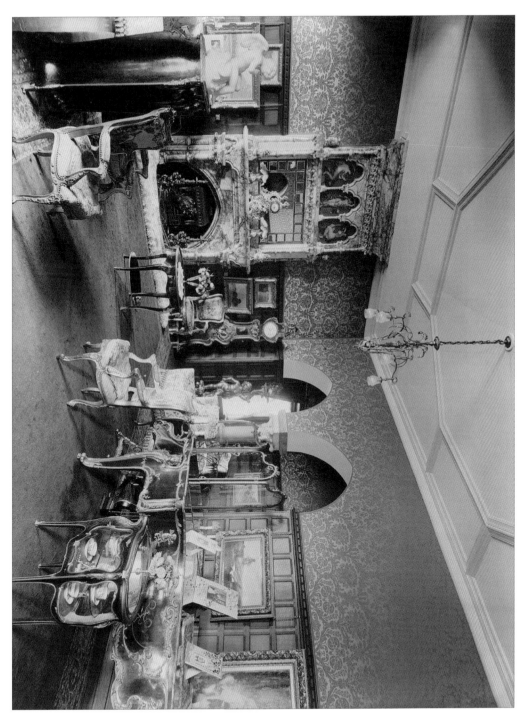

Fig 98: Harry Bedford Lemere photograph of the drawing room, the bay window to the left (out of frame) provides the light. July 1904.

Anne's brother Jack Garrett and his wife Mary along with their children Esme, Zaidee and Lennox.

This branch of the family occupied the tower rooms, which were spacious enough to accommodate them with ease. John Brown (who later adopted his mother's maiden name) used to also sometimes stay at the house. He was the son of Florence Jesson, a schoolfriend of Anne Hollins. She had taken a liking to the young boy and had paid for his education.

The move was not without difficulty - principally the problem of furnishing such a large place - and the family employed twelve servants, including a butler and housekeeper, supplemented by a range of cooks and maids together with three gardeners who ensured a ready supply of fruit, flowers and vegetables for the household. Soon after moving in, Mrs Hollins caught pneumonia apparently as a result of the dampness in the house. Complications set in and she died on 26th January 1926.

Despite the premature death of their mother, the Hollins boys seemed to have enjoyed their years at the house. To counteract the damp and cold, a hot-air heating system was installed at Milner Field, with a grate in the hall. The fresh water to the house was pumped through a

Fig 99: Anne Hollins.   *Fig 100: Arthur Remington Hollins.*

ram and, though the lake was clear (and Arthur Hollins had toyed with the idea of draining it to see what fish stocks remained) the family never boated on it.

The late Dick Hollins, with whom we spoke in 1998, remembered that his father had brought with him senior members of staff from previous houses including a head parlour

*This excellent series of photographs
from the Hollins period taken in
or near the courtyard give a good
impression of the privileges and
lifestyle enjoyed by the children of
the wealthy.*

*Fun in the courtyard:
clockwise from above.*

Fig 101: By home-made sledge.

*Fig 102: Dick and Ted Hollins on
motorcycles, Brough model on the
left, 26th August 1927.*

*Fig 103: Entering the courtyard in a
Bugatti type 38.*

*Fig 104: Posing in front of the gates.
(L-R) John Brown (Jesson), Dick
Hollins and Ted Hollins at the wheel
of his Bentley
three litre open
tourer.*

Fig 105: Left. Dick Hollins and a partially-obscured Arthur Hollins in the Milner Field dining room.

Fig 106: Right. Photograph from the Hollins period showing the drawing room bay window and orangery leading into the eastern end of the conservatory.

Fig 107: Three little residents of the tower rooms, L-R, Esme, Lennox and Zaidee Garrett.

Fig 108: North terrace view, from the Hollins' period (compare with Fig: 124).

Fig: 109. Above left. Dick Hollins by the Gothic arch.

Fig: 110. Above right. In the courtyard porch. Ted Hollins (left) and unknown friend.

Fig: 111. Left. Ted Hollins' Bentley at the Gothic arch, September 1929.

Fig: 112. Below. Arthur Hollins, with an unnamed liberal politician, seated against the west wall of the conservatory at Milner Field.

Fig 113: Above. Park front view of the house and conservatory.

Fig 114: Left. L-R. Ted Hollins, Dick Hollins and family friend John Brown (Jesson) standing next to the courtyard gates.

Fig 115: Below. Car leaving Milner Field courtyard through the Gothic arch.

Fig 116: Hollins era view of the south front.

maid called Gertrude and their chauffeur, Austin. Gertrude was in the habit of writing out the day's dinner menu on a china plate and caused a little consternation one day when she described the main course as "*roast lion of lamb*"! Though they spent much of their time away at school, Dick Hollins recalled lacking companionship at the house as his brother was four years his elder. Arthur Hollins, unlike Titus Jnr, enjoyed rural pursuits such as fishing and shooting and amassed an amazing cellar which included what Dick described as a "*hundred dozen bottles ... a pipe of port*". Whether, as was common among some affluent English families, the pipe of port (thought to be roughly one hundred and thirty eight wine gallons) was laid down at the birth of a son only to be released on his twenty-first birthday, is unclear. After Arthur Hollins' death, the cellar was split between his brothers. Milner Field had plenty of room for visitors and it would appear that they were treated rather well. Tennis could be played on a court which was laid out on the site of the former Milner Field. Dick also remembered the former stable block near the north lodge being used to house the family's cars as they owned no horses. Guests' cars were always washed and filled with petrol from Milner Field's own pump before they departed!

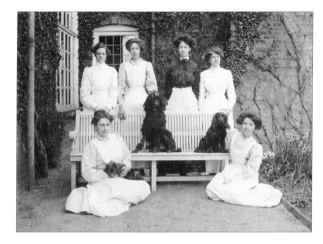

Like Gates before him, Hollins was only fifty-one when he died. He had previously enjoyed good health, but in 1929 on a summer holiday with his sons to the north of Scotland he was taken ill and admitted to a nursing home in Edinburgh.

Fig 117: Members of the Hollins household staff, with family pets, at a previous house. Gertrude, head parlour maid, is standing on the extreme right.

His sudden death was caused by irritation of the gall-bladder, liver and diaphragm, leading to unstoppable hiccoughs. A patient with this exhausting condition was normally sedated, but this was felt to be inappropriate in Hollins' case and so he literally hiccoughed to death. His funeral service took place at Bingley Parish Church on 19th August and interment followed, beside his late wife, at Nab Wood cemetery.

Fig 118: This superb photograph of the southern aspect of the house dates from the Hollins era.

White Elephant

In 1930 Hollins' sons left Milner Field for Ilkley and the Salts company determined to rid itself of the house, whose reputation for despatching its occupants to a premature grave was now rendering the place decidedly unattractive. A second sale catalogue was drawn up but, once again, it failed to sell and the house was closed up, never again to be the home of a director of Salts.

Throughout the 1930s the house stood empty, with occasional rumours in the press of possible new uses under consideration. It was mooted that it would make an excellent future University of Bradford at one stage, though the idea of Bradford Corporation buying the place was scorned as profligate in the letters pages of the local newspapers.

Fig 119: Photograph of the north aspect of the house with the ivy covered courtyard wall and archway in the foreground.

Fig 120: Above: Detail of the oriel window, with its stepped corbel, during the Hollins occupancy.
Fig 121: Below: By the 1950s the orangery and conservatory had gone. The house was now used
as a ready source of materials to patch up the mill.

Comparatively little is known of the house at this time. During the war years, with raw materials such as timber and slates in short supply, chargehands from the mill were often sent to cannibalise the house for repair material. The temptation to plunder the kitchen gardens of their soft fruits was also seldom resisted. Local children used the marble floors of the once-magnificent conservatory as an impromptu roller-skating rink and they were not alone in putting the place to an alternative use - the Home Guard also pressed it into service as a makeshift rifle range, though one hopes that the visits of these respective parties never overlapped!

Around the time of the outbreak of the Second World War, it is rumoured the gates under the gothic arch were taken down. This was presumably to foil the plans of the scrap iron dealers who were charged with taking down gates and railings on public and private property alike to aid the country's war effort. A further and more intriguing rumour alludes to the fact that a later Managing Director ordered the gates be rehung on a private house in the locality and, we are assured, they hang there to this day with their history presumably unknown to the householder! Frustratingly, their exact location has not been disclosed.

The contradictions which can plague the historian's research arise again when we turn our attention to the fate of the conservatory. Two local people who contacted the authors gave differing accounts. One remembers a local scrap merchant cutting the massive structure down in 1940. Interestingly, local man Barry Wood who moved to the area in 1946, distinctly remembers the conservatory being "*largely intact*" in the immediate post war years when he and his friends would roller skate in it and he recalled its marble floor being ideal for this purpose. His recollections seem particularly accurate as he also states that the glazing was still in place and wrily comments that "*modern children would have wrecked [it] but we just enjoyed our roller skating*"[36]. He pinpoints his memories to around 1948 and as a teenager recalled seeing the sun glinting off the glass as he gazed from his bedroom window across the valley toward Milner Field. Certainly no trace of the conservatory remains, save the stone footings, by the time the house was photographed from the air by C.H. Wood on 18th August 1949. (See Figs 161 and 162).

As the reader will have seen, much of interest has been written about this great house during the decades when it provided a backdrop to the lives of the wealthy and powerful. While it was still used as a family home, its history is somewhat easier to trace. Records exist, careers can be charted, and photographs can be often unearthed. When a house is abandoned, the task of the historian is made that much more difficult. Much of the information we have gathered from the years 1930 onwards is rich in detail but poor on dates.

Fig 122: Detail of marble fireplace.

The human memory being what it is, if no personal landmark event exists on which to hang a particular recollection then the memory can become clouded. Contradictory dates and reminiscences are by no means uncommon and though they are given in all sincerity it can be a frustrating exercise attempting to untangle them. We are, therefore, particularly grateful to those who answered our pleas for information and could do so either with the aid of tangible evidence - be it a cutting or photograph - or by reliance on a sharp memory, undimmed by the passing years.

Ghostly Goings-on

Bradford man, Trevor Meek, recalls that curious locals continued to be attracted by the forlorn and eerie structure. In the early 1940s, he and his friend Fred visited the ruins one moonlit night. Fresh from a trip to the cinema, the boys' heads were still full of another chilling old mansion: Manderlay in Hitchcock's film of Daphne du Maurier's *Rebecca*. Though many of the floorboards had been taken up at Milner Field, the moonlight enabled the boys to explore safely, and they entered the drawing room, which Trevor remembers was decorated in a pale duck-egg blue. Venturing further around the ruins (the roofs, he remembers, had gone by this time) they decided to investigate the domestic wing where the kitchens and dairy lay. As luck would have it, clouds scudded across the bright moon at this moment, making what had seemed a clear way suddenly treacherous. Momentarily disorientated, Trevor lost his footing and fell down a flight of steps towards the deep cellars. Unhurt he started to clamber back up as the moon re-appeared, reflecting off the flooded basement which lay below and which could so easily have claimed him. *"We ran off like mad down the drive",* he recalled in 1998, *"and that was that adventure over with!"*[37]

In the years immediately following the war, the house's gaunt remains lost none of their allure.

We are grateful to Mr Peter Horne who sent us a page from the *Salt High School Magazine* of December 1947. One of his fellow classmates, D. W. Ellis, had written a wistful account of a visit to the ruins and which is useful in ascertaining the state of the house in the immediate aftermath of the war.

Fig 123: It is as well that Titus Jnr did not live to see the house he loved become an unwanted ruin, its ultimate fate, demolition.

"If any traveller should happen to make his way along the winding, hedge-bound lane locally termed "The Carriage Drive," he would eventually arrive at a shady avenue leading to a pair of gates guarded by a lodge. Although the estate entered by these gates is private, the inoffensive visitor should meet small difficulty in satisfying his curiosity regarding the nature of it. When he entered the gate he would proceed along a winding path shaded by a canopy of trees with luxuriant vegetation on either side, now, alas, little better than a wilderness. The drive, crumbling and moss-grown, is only one of the signs that point the progress of decay.

The most impressive spectacle offered is held, like the greatest actor in a play, until the beholder has become accustomed to the prevailing atmosphere. It is the ruined mansion of Milner Field. Turning a bend in the path, the traveller finds himself gazing on the shell of this palatial edifice.

A huge archway marks the entrance into a small yard, but all round lie discarded stones, broken glass and fittings. As one moves about, one sees gutted windows, skeletons of floors, an outhouse (of which only two walls stand), much beautiful tilework, a huge ornamented fireplace and carved chimney stacks – a work of art to behold. Across the front of the house runs a verandah, from which a flight of steps descends. It is overgrown with weeds, and the summer-house at one end has been almost entirely destroyed.

Fig 124: Milner Field from the north terrace, late 19th century.

Yet, to a contemplative beholder, it is not difficult to imagine the mansion's ancient splendour. The time when a great fire blazed in the ornate marble fireplace, and well-sprung carriages rolled in under the great archway. It is not hard to imagine the festive scene in the candle-lit hall, or the cheerful throng which must have promenaded on the verandah or rested in the pleasant summer-house. Or another scene which might present itself to him. Perhaps the owner, awakened by the neighbouring throstles, taking a ride over the nearby park-land some summer morn before breakfast.

Leaving this impressive scene, the observer may continue his way along the path, until he approaches another gate guarded by another quaint lodge, through which he may pass from this decaying wilderness of the nineteenth century into the busy, hurried life of the present day."

In August 1951, the house gained ghostly credentials when fifteen year old Anthony Davis of Bingley told the *Bingley Guardian* of his encounter with an apparition near the tower rooms.

Level-headed Anthony, who went on to become a journalist himself, came face to face with an apparition carrying a flute and dressed in green Edwardian clothes amid the ruins of the house – this sighting was to give rise to talk of "*The Green Man of Milner Field*" which persists to this day.

Fig 125: A 1950s winter image of the partially ruined house seen through the still intact courtyard entrance arch.

Under the headline "Gilstead Boy's Eerie Experience", the article ran: *"Listen for a moment to Anthony's story of what happened to him one evening recently when he was exploring the ruins of Milner Field, Bingley, former residence of Mr Titus Salt.*

It was about 7.30pm, says Anthony, when he picked his way over fallen bricks and mortar, and made his way to the old turret room.

It is true that the place is in a sad state of dilapidation, but the scene was hardly set for apparitions; after all it was high summer and not a season one usually associates with ghostly visitations.

Consequently Anthony, who is head boy at Bingley Modern School was not at first particularly concerned when from a room (or the remains of a room) at his right there stepped a man garbed in green.

The man paused for a moment in front of Anthony, and then moved away into the apartment on his left. Over the broken-down fireplace of this room Anthony saw a mirror – and his own reflection – but not that of the man in green. He was unnerved and even more so when the mirror 'misted' away and the man vanished too!

Stories of this kind inevitably arouse scepticism, but Anthony seems a remarkably well-balanced lad, and he told me the story with an impressive matter-of-factness.

"You have, of course, a vivid imagination" I suggested. "Not particularly vivid", he replied.

And certainly over the fireplace are marks of where a mirror has been. I asked Anthony if he could remember anything specific about the man in green. He replied that he could not with accuracy but formed the decided impression that his clothing was Edwardian. "They were certainly not modern," he said flatly. "He carried a musical instrument under his arm, something resembling a flute. He was hatless and his hair was matted".

And then Anthony shuddered. He said there was the smell of something indescribably offensive. "What did you do after both the mirror and the man disappeared?" I asked.

Anthony smiled bleakly, "Ran for my life" he admitted ruefully. Later with two of his friends, he returned to the ruined building, but investigations yielded nothing. Anthony tells me that some people claim to have found broken glass in the room but he rather discounted this as evidence.

Certainly one could imagine Milner Fields [sic] as a happy hunting ground for spectres and probably a scrutiny of the records might reveal a gory tale.

Particularly is this so of the building that stood there prior to its demolition in 1860 [sic]. At an early date, reveals Harry Speight's Chronicles and Stories of Bingley and District, the place belonged to the old Bingley family of Mylner or Milner, who settled there at the time of Richard II. In 1869 the estate was sold by Admiral Duncombe to the late Mr Titus Salt for a sum in the region of £21,000"[38].

It is interesting to note that Anthony, who has sadly since died, apparently never wavered from, nor added to, his very sober account throughout his life and the Green Man of Milner Field joined the folklore surrounding the house.

Oddly, we had our own strange experience in the grounds of the house whilst researching this book. As we wanted to measure the site, and the footings that marked the remains of the billiard room in particular, we had taken along with us a professional surveyor's tape measure in a leather case. This was of the old type that had to be wound-in by hand using a crank handle on the side of the case and it was a little stiff and uncooperative. As the billiard room was sizeable – some thirty feet in length - we secured one end of the measure on the remains of a brick wall while we extended the tape across the room. When this task was completed – but while the tape was still fully extended – we broke off briefly to speak to an elderly gentleman who had stopped to talk to us. We must add at this point

Fig 126: Excellent study of the conservatory, or Palm House as it was described in the manufacturer's brochure. This structure was supplied and erected by Walter Macfarlane & Co, Saracen Foundry, Glasgow. It is unusual in that the solid west end wall is shown.

that the area was otherwise deserted and silent: we would certainly have noticed had any prankster wandered on to the site at this time. We chatted with the man for a few minutes before clambering back over the remains to retrieve the tape measure only to find that it had completely disappeared! The pair of us searched the billiard room remains exhaustively but without success. Scratching our heads with incredulity, we repeated our search but this proved equally fruitless. We had just about given it up as lost when we spotted the missing measure, its thirty feet of tape fully and neatly rewound, hanging by its loop from the branch of a tree which had grown through the remains of the room. The branch from which it was hanging was roughly twelve feet from the ground – way beyond the reach of most people – and it took some precarious shinning-up and balancing to successfully retrieve it. How this occurred mystified us at the time and continues to do so to this day. The very act of winding up the tape, let alone the almost superhuman effort of hanging it from so high a branch, would have taken quite some time to execute, not to mention a certain agility, and we were left clueless as to who or what was responsible for this strange incident.

Declining Years

Though the precise date of its demise is uncertain, it is clear that by the early 1950s a decision to demolish the house had been reached.

Local man, Bob MacDonald, knew the house for much of his working life as he started work for Salts in the late 1920s as an apprentice joiner. Bob's vivid memories have added greatly to our knowledge of Milner Field. He recalls one of his first tasks was to batten together some 15ft long lengths of white wood into which holes were cut. These were then placed over pails and used as makeshift lavatories for a group of blind children who were taken up to the house by a local charity in order to enjoy the spacious grounds. As the years passed he recalls workers from the mill being sent to the house to collect the soft fruits which grew in abundance in the kitchen gardens.

Older readers will remember that in the years immediately following the end of the Second World War many resources were still in short supply (in fact citizens couldn't tear up their ration books until the summer of 1954!) and the make-do-and-mend mentality borne of wartime austerity still prevailed, with permits for certain materials still being required. It has been suggested to us by local people interviewed for this book that the house was used as a source of some raw materials for the mill – an example cited being that if high winds caused the loss of some slates from the combing shed roof, a ready supply of replacements could be found at the empty and closed-up Milner Field. Trevor Meek thought the roofs had disappeared by the time of his visit in the very early 1940s. Bob's recollections though seem to run at variance with this as he remembers the house, right up until the time of its eventual demolition, as being a "warm, snug, dry place"[39] which it most certainly would not have been had its roofs been the subject of repeated raids. On 29th January 1947, the Shipley Times & Express describes the house as "internally practically demolished". Photographs from around the immediate postwar period show the house roofless. Some observers have commented that a fire may have been responsible for this. We have found nothing to support this and certainly the building does not bear the characteristic tell-tale signs of smoke/fire damage; for instance no charred beams or trusses can be seen – it does look as if the whole roof structure was removed. It seems, then, more likely to surmise that the removal of the roofs rendered the building no longer liable to rates, as has been suggested to us, and that a cost-saving exercise of this nature acted to accelerate the decline of Milner Field.

It is certainly the case though that when a decision was reached to pull down Milner Field, Bob and other maintenance workers from the mill were sent there to begin the stripping-out work. Bob, with his love of wood, particularly remembered the beautiful chestnut and French walnut panelling which was removed and which was later utilised for partitions and other sundry uses in the mill. The broad wooden floorboards with their metal tongue and grooving were taken up, though the joists were left. The ornate handrail from the staircase, with its carved and hammered leaf decoration, was carefully removed and languished in the cellars of the mill for many years in the hope that a new use could be found for it. Opposite the bottom of the staircase Bob remembers a huge mural painted on the wall depicting a white charger rearing up on its hind legs. Intrigued by this recollection, we showed him the only similar picture in our possession showing the hunting mural which adorned the wall of the billiard room but strangely this was not what he recalled, so we can only assume that Bob's horse was a later artistic addition and was never caught for posterity by the camera.

Figs 127 & 128: Left. David Beale, clearing the overgrown floor of the conservatory in 2005 to reveal traces of the mosaic floor. Inset: Mosaic detail. Right. Kerb edging to beds still exists.

Bob's memories paint a vivid picture of the house in its declining years – Teddy Hollins manoeuvring his enormous silver Bugatti up the carriage drive to the courtyard as it was so big it couldn't be turned around anywhere else; the house's many bathrooms each with a heavy telephone at the foot of the bath, suggesting that at least some of the later Managing Directors may have had some of their best ideas while soaking in the tub!; the body of one of the later Managing Directors, incongruously, lying "in state" in the house's store room while mourners paid their respects; the lake well-stocked with Loch Levan trout, some of which – to the villagers' evident delight – often made their way into the river; the dairy with its scrubbed white hexagonal table; the wild dog that had taken up residence in the drawing room; the ferrets despatched into the boiler-house's labyrinth of pipes after rabbits; the echoing rooms with their magnificent marble fireplaces still intact and a chauffeur who lived in the bottom (or South) lodge and shared the surname of the Managing Director and about whom we can only assume some Hollins-related confusion may well have arisen!

Bob's contact with the house after the war was sporadic as his work obviously centred around the mill and its closely-associated buildings. He and his colleagues would attend after the occasional break-in and make good the burglar's means of entry. He remembers one day repairing an area of flat roof between two pitched ones near the orangery after lead had been stolen and gallons of accumulated rainwater were threatening to plunge through. The glory days of Milner Field had clearly drawn to a close and ahead of it lay only ruin

Fig 129: Splendid study of the conservatory's interior (showing greater detail, such as ceiling lights and central heating radiators) taken from 'Examples of Macfarlane's Architectural Ironwork' which was issued c1922 but which contains illustrations of buildings known to have been constructed from the 1890s onwards. This pair of intriguing images (Figs 126 & 129) carry no specific date, but would appear to be from the Roberts era, and appears courtesy of the Scottish Ironwork Foundation.

and desolation. The beginning of the end was reached one grim day when maintenance workers from the mill piled their trucks high with fine panelling and woodwork in the courtyard that had once been graced by royalty. It was laborious work – one can safely assume the Victorians never had demolition in mind – as the parquet floor set in pitch, and metal tongued and grooved floorboards were ripped up and the house, which until then had been in a remarkably fair state of preservation, was closed up again.

The dilapidated house began to attract vandals and thieves and stones from the archway and outbuildings were gradually stolen, as Figs 157 and 160 confirm.

Amid concerns over, or perhaps on the pretext of, safety, a gang from Bolton Woods quarries were sent to lay charges and bring the whole decaying edifice crashing down. The team of masons took the best part of two days to drill out the house's substantial foundations and lay their explosive charges. Bob recalls clearly the crisp autumn morning when he, his late brother Hector, Group Engineer Jack Heaton and the workmen huddled behind the remains of the Gothic arch to plunge the detonator. A great roar rent the air and, when the dust had settled, they were amazed to see the house still standing and, to all appearances, unaffected by the explosion. A testament, if one were needed, to the muscularity of Harris' design!

The ruins of the house remained, though the Gothic arch was itself blown up (after another ineffective first attempt) some time later. Gradually, what was left of the house fell prey to the elements and thieves and sometime later the site must have been cleared. Harry Downs, whose family have farmed Milner Field Farm for many decades, recalled in 1996 that "*it was blown up for safety reasons, about 1957, and was left in a heap; most of the stone was stolen*"[40]. There may be readers who can add more to our knowledge of this period and contact through our publishers would certainly be welcome (see page 98).

Epilogue

Walking through the ruins of Milner Field today, it is difficult not to be consumed by great feelings of sadness and loss. The cellars lie gaping to the skies, their brick-vaulted ceilings, though now inaccessible, still in a fine state of preservation while lichen and grass push through the once fine mosaic of the conservatory. There, amid the densely growing trees, brush and weeds stand many monumental, displaced pieces of masonry. Some are boldly carved, some just anonymous courses of brickwork. Together they stand in mute testimony to a family and a lifestyle which has long since disappeared. Truly a vanished age.

The ruins also serve to remind the observer of something else: that we do not have freehold rights on our heritage. It has often been said that we are only caretakers for future generations and that, to us falls the responsibility of ensuring that those who follow us can explore their roots, historically, socially and architecturally. Perhaps it is a high-flown ideal and it would indeed be a foolish person who imagined that everything of note from the past could be preserved for the future. But it is scarcely possible to argue that we are not, as a nation, much the poorer following the loss of so many great buildings and monuments. Broadening our scope for a moment, can Londoners, for example, truly be said to have profited by the replacement in 1962 of their splendid, towering Euston Arch - seventy feet of granite in Grecian style symbolising the grandeur and innovation of rail travel - with a vulgar railway concourse and windswept car park?

We are in many ways more fortunate now. The sense of possession, even curatorship, in society is becoming more pronounced and the casual destruction, so commonplace only fifty years ago, is now not only met with vocal moral indignation but is in many cases outlawed by a raft of preservation orders and listed building regulations.

Clambering unsteadily among the overgrown remains of the house recently, we reached the area where the elegant drawing room once stood. As we surveyed the rubble, we were reminded of a letter to Catherine Salt in the Salt family's private archive. Mrs Salt, as we saw earlier, was making preparations for the fancy dress ball to be held in the autumn of 1895 at which her daughter Isabel was to be "brought out". The firm of Womersley and Company (Public Decorators and Bazaar Contractors) in Leeds had been instructed to provide sumptuous amber and cream art drapery, to supply and warm seating for the guests and to lay polished parquet floors. The widowed Mrs Salt, understandably proprietorial, was at pains to ensure no damage was caused to the fabric of the room. In their reply, the firm assured her "*we will undertake to use the utmost care. The joists will be laid on pieces of felt, so they will not touch the floor [and] we should leave a space of ¼ inch up to the wainscot, to avoid scratching*"[41]. It is indeed poignant to think that a house, whose construction and upkeep during its heady years was marked by loving attention to detail and painstaking care, should end its days an embattled shell, open to the elements, cannibalised, dynamited and eventually ripped apart, stone from stone.

If nothing else, Milner Field should serve as a reminder that no matter how noble, cultured and lofty man's ideals, their undoing through a combination of shifting fortunes, neglect and the tides of fashion is both swift and irrevocable.

Notes

1. La Page *Story of Baildon*, 1951.

2. Harris, John *No voice from the hall: early memories of a country house snooper*, John Murray, 1998.

3. Ibid.

4. *Bradford Observer*, 6th December 1866.

5. Speight, Harry *Chronicles and stories of old Bingley: a full account of the history, antiquities,natural productions, scenery, customs and folk-lore of the ancient town of Bingley, in the West Riding of Yorkshire* Elliot Stock, London, 1898.

6. Reid, T. Wemyss *The Life of The Rt Hon William Edward Forster*, 1888.

7. Balgarnie, Reverend Robert *Sir Titus Salt, Baronet: His Life and its Lessons*, 1878 (reprinted with commentary and additons by Barlo & Shaw, Nemine Juvante (Saltaire) Publications, 2003).

8. Harbron, Dudley *Thomas Harris* (essay in) *Architectural Review*, Volume 92, September 1942.

9. Harris, Thomas *Three Periods of English Architecture*, 1894.

10. Harris, Thomas *Victorian Architecture*, 1860.

11. Ibid.

12. *Milner Field Estate, Saltaire, Yorkshire.* (Sale Catalogue.) A. Gadie & Son, Bradford, 1922.

13. Healey *A series of picturesque views of castles and country houses in Yorkshire*, 1885.

14.Harris, Thomas *Victorian Architecture*, 1860.

15.Saunderson, Rosemary Claire *Titus Salt of Milner Field: a study in nineteenth century industrial taste*, Leeds 1993.

16. *Building News*, 22nd December 1876.

17. *Shipley & Saltaire Times*, 24th November 1877.

18. Idem. (Speight).

19. Vance, Peggy *William Morris Wallpapers*, Bracken Books, 1989.

20. Interview with authors, 30th August 1996

21. Payne, B & D *Extracts from the journal of John Deakin Heaton* in The Thoresby Miscellany, Volume 15, Leeds 1972.

22. *Shipley & Saltaire Times*, 15th September 1877.

23. Ibid.

24. *Shipley & Saltaire Times*, 20th September 1879.

25. *Shipley Times*, 7th May 1887.

26. *Bradford Observer*, 29th November 1887.

27. Bolton, Sybil & Glorney *Two Lives Converge: the dual autobiography of Sybil and Glorney Bolton*, Blackie & Son, London, 1938.

28. Contract between Mrs Catherine Salt & James Roberts Esquire relating to the sale of Milner Field Estate, 17th January 1903.

29. Idem (Bolton).

30. Ibid.

31. Bill Tegner - correspondence with the authors, 17th July 1999.

32. *Yorkshire Evening Argus*, 30th August, 1925.

33. *Yorkshire Observer*, 2nd April 1925.

34. http://www.leighrayment.Com/commons/Mcommons2.htm

35. *Mansfield Reporter*, 16th October 1925.

36. Barry Wood, correspondence with the authors, 4th August 1996.

37. Trevor Meek, interview with the authors, 30th August 1996.

38. *Bingley Guardian*, 31st August 1951.

39. Bob MacDonald, interview with the authors, 3rd August 1996.

40. Harry Downs, correspondence, 23rd July 1996.

41. Letter to Catherine Salt, dated August 1895.

Suggested further reading

Girouard, Mark *The Victorian Country House* (Yale University Press, 1979)

Harris, John *No voice from the hall: early memories of a country house snooper* (Murray, 1998)

Linstrum, Derek *West Yorkshire architects and architecture* (Lund Humphries, 1978)

Pevsner, Nikolaus and Leach, Peter *The buildings of England: Yorkshire West Riding, Leeds, Bradford and the North* (Yale University Press, 2009)

Waterson, Edward and Meadows, Peter *Lost houses of the West Riding* (Jill Raines Publishing, 1998)

Sheeran, George *Brass Castles: West Yorkshire new rich and their houses 1800-1914* (Ryburn Publishing Limited, 1993)

Film.

The Story of Saltaire. Barleybrookfilms.co.uk

Contact may be made with the publishers through the following sites:

http://www.milner-field.co.uk

http://www.barleybrookfilms.co.uk

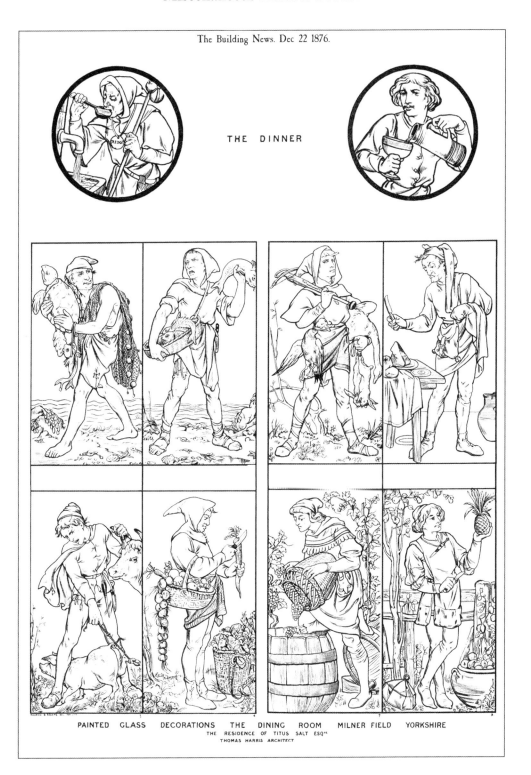

Fig 130: The Dinner. This outstanding stained glass panel depicting a romanticised view of medieval peasants was one of several works by Frederick Weekes which adorned the rooms of Milner Field.

Fig 131: Photograph from the 1880s of Catherine Salt wearing the exquisite pearl gown, which can be seen as it is today in Figs 91-92.

Fig 132: Detail of the remains of the base of one of the old Milner Field gate posts. See Figs 14, 16, 27 and 93.

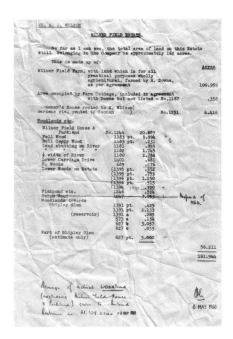

Fig 133: Document dated 6th May 1960 reporting on the amount of land still owned by the company, presumably Illingworth Morris.

Fig 134: Unknown woman modelling the Mary Queen of Scots dress (see also fig 90).

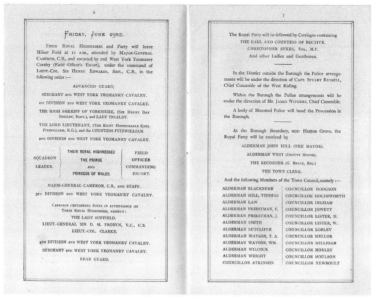

*Fig 135: The evening recital programme from the
1882 Royal visit.*

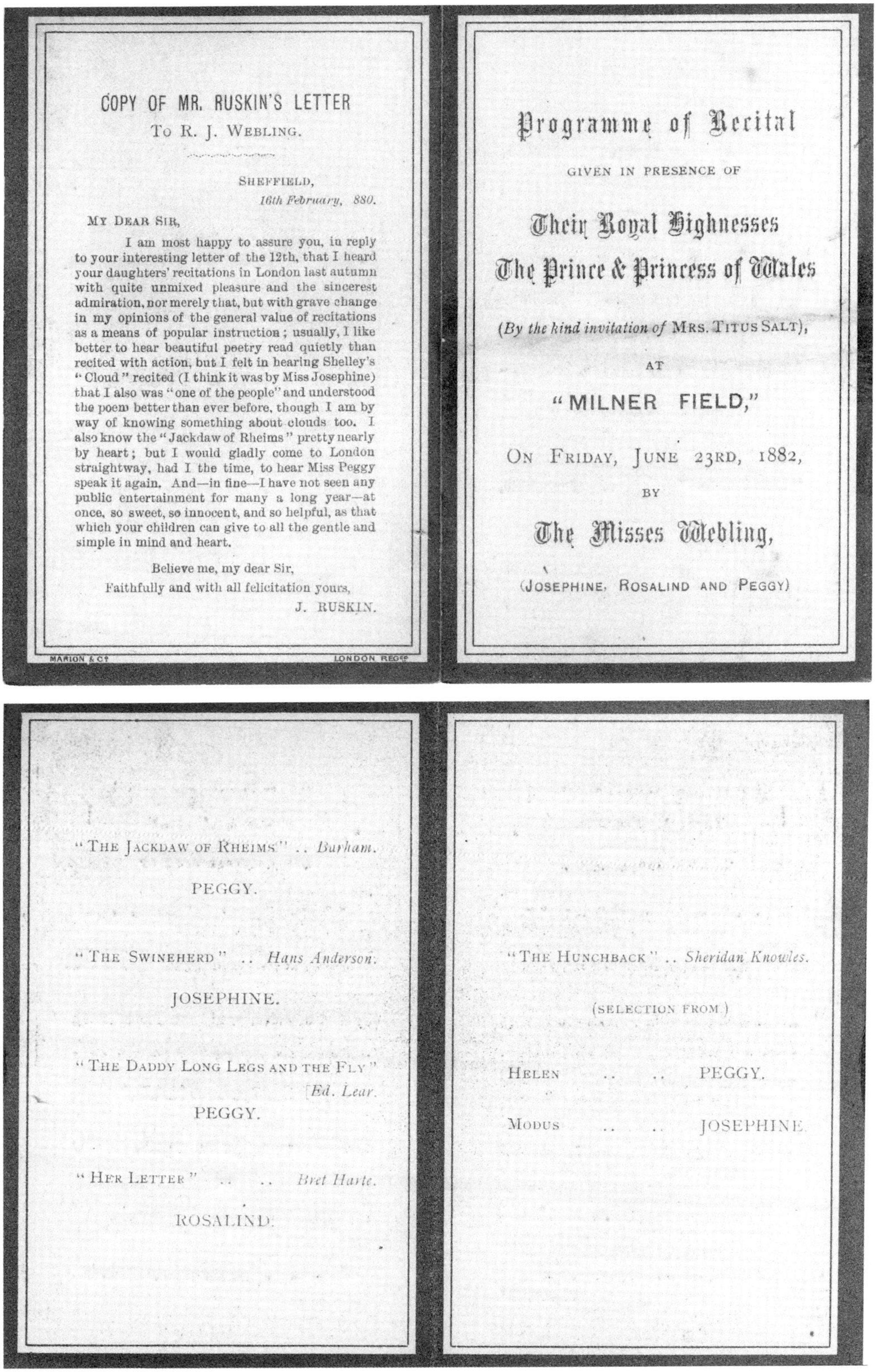

COPY OF MR. RUSKIN'S LETTER

To R. J. WEBLING.

SHEFFIELD,
16th February, 880.

MY DEAR SIR,

I am most happy to assure you, in reply to your interesting letter of the 12th, that I heard your daughters' recitations in London last autumn with quite unmixed pleasure and the sincerest admiration, nor merely that, but with grave change in my opinions of the general value of recitations as a means of popular instruction; usually, I like better to hear beautiful poetry read quietly than recited with action, but I felt in hearing Shelley's " Cloud " recited (I think it was by Miss Josephine) that I also was "one of the people" and understood the poem better than ever before, though I am by way of knowing something about clouds too. I also know the " Jackdaw of Rheims " pretty nearly by heart; but I would gladly come to London straightway, had I the time, to hear Miss Peggy speak it again. And—in fine—I have not seen any public entertainment for many a long year—at once, so sweet, so innocent, and so helpful, as that which your children can give to all the gentle and simple in mind and heart.

Believe me, my dear Sir,

Faithfully and with all felicitation yours,

J. RUSKIN.

MARION & Cᵒ   LONDON REGᵈ

Programme of Recital

GIVEN IN PRESENCE OF

Their Royal Highnesses
The Prince & Princess of Wales

(*By the kind invitation of* MRS. TITUS SALT),

AT

" MILNER FIELD,"

ON FRIDAY, JUNE 23RD, 1882,

BY

The Misses Webling,

(JOSEPHINE, ROSALIND AND PEGGY)

" THE JACKDAW OF RHEIMS " .. *Barham.*

PEGGY.

" THE SWINEHERD " .. *Hans Anderson.*

JOSEPHINE.

" THE DADDY LONG LEGS AND THE FLY "
[*Ed. Lear.*

PEGGY.

" HER LETTER " .. .. *Bret Harte.*

ROSALIND.

" THE HUNCHBACK " .. *Sheridan Knowles.*

(SELECTION FROM)

HELEN .. .. PEGGY.

MODUS .. .. JOSEPHINE.

---

*Fig 136: The evening recital programme
from the 1882 Royal visit.*

Fig 137: Isabel, Catherine's youngest child, dressed for a portrait.

Fig 138: Isabel on her pony "Bess" in the courtyard at Milner Field.

One of the gateway lights can be made out against the ivy.

*Fig 139: Looking eastwards through the arched gateway of the courtyard.
The base of the lamp on the left column can be seen in Fig 138.*

*Fig 140: Looking westwards to where the arched gateway stood, little remains
of this once elegant and stately edifice. c 1970s.*

Fig 141: This superb marble bust of Titus Jnr is part of the Salt collection at Lotherton Hall, Leeds.

Fig 142: This 2004 image shows the nderside of the domestic staircase, which led from the main house to the kitchen wing. It is still in remarkably good order.

Fig 143: A 'Votes for Women' group photographed in the Milner Field conservatory. Green, white and violet sashes (the initial letters standing for "Give Women Votes") signified the peaceful campaign. Isabel can be seen at the front, while Catherine is to the rear right, behind young Lawrence who seems to have been drafted in for the occasion.

Fig 144: Left. Portrait of Gordon Salt aged five in a sailor's outfit, seen in situ in the drawing room in Fig 43.

Fig 145: Above. Studio portrait of Gordon as a young man.

Fig 146: Below. Gordon and Florence on their wedding day in 1903. She was the daughter of the vicar of Rossington in South Yorkshire.

Fig 147: Below. Gordon in later life.

Fig 148: Gordon Salt and friends in a posed, jokey shot relaxing in the conservatory. The carefully-staged debauchery might have been aimed at irritating Gordon's mother!

Fig 149: Below. Detail of a column capital in the hall. See also Fig 49.

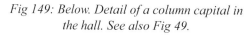

Fig 150: Below. Detail of the same column capital lying amongst the rubble of Milner Field in the 1960s.

Fig 151: Above left. During 2008 the North Lodge underwent a complete renovation. This image shows the early stages of the work.

Fig 152: Above. An extension has been added to the lodge, the style and quality of the stonework are completely in keeping with the original property.

Fig 153: Above and Fig 154: Right.

These two images of the North Lodge show the restoration complete.

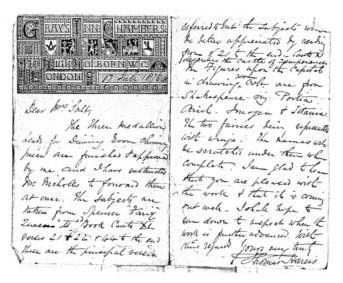

Fig 155: Letter from Thomas Harris, the architect of Milner Field, to Mrs Salt, July 1876.

Fig 156: Detail of the column capital with its Shakespearian reliefs, referred to by Thomas Harris in the letter above. See also Fig 45.

Fig 157: A 1959 image of a derelict Milner Field, seen through the collapsed courtyard Gothic arch.

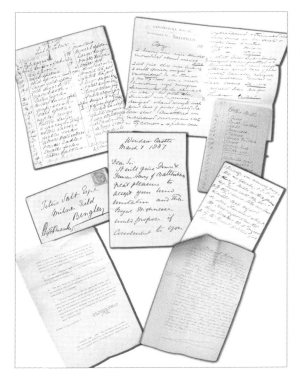

Fig 158: Left. Various pieces of correspondence and other documents from the extensive Salt family archives.

Fig 159: Below. Invitation with attached gilded pencil for Isabel's coming out party in 1895.

Fig 160: The remains in March 1961, taken by 15 year old John Irwin, the continuing rate of decay is clear when compared with Fig 157.

Fig 161: Above. This amazing photograph was found shortly before completion of this book and was taken by C.H. Wood on 18th August 1949. It came to light during cataloguing of the C.H.Wood photographic collection held by the Bradford Industrial Museum and is shown here for the first time.

Fig 162: This close-up image of the roofless house clearly shows much of the interior.
The Gothic arch, courtyard and orangery are all clearly visible. It is possible that the roof was
deliberately removed to avoid council rates.

Fig 163: Portrait photograph of Isabel taken during a visit to Kelso.

Fig 164: The old rectory at Thorp Arch. Catherine Salt lived here after Denton Park

Fig 165: Portrait photograph of Lawrence and Isabel.

Fig 166: Titus Jnr, aged two.

Part of the Christopher Hand collection, held by the Bradford Industrial Museum

Images from the 1960s.

Fig 167: Above. Site of the conservatory.

Fig 168: Above right. Filled in passageway and elaborate stone door casing.

Fig 169: Below. The remains of the base of the round garden house. See Fig 25.

Figs: 170, 171, 172 & 173.

Images of the North Lodge from the 1960s.

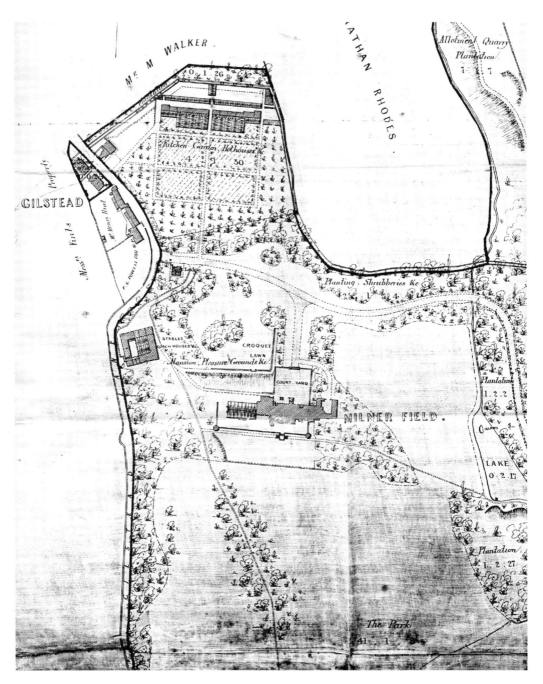

Fig 174: 19th century sketch plan of part of the Milner Field estate.

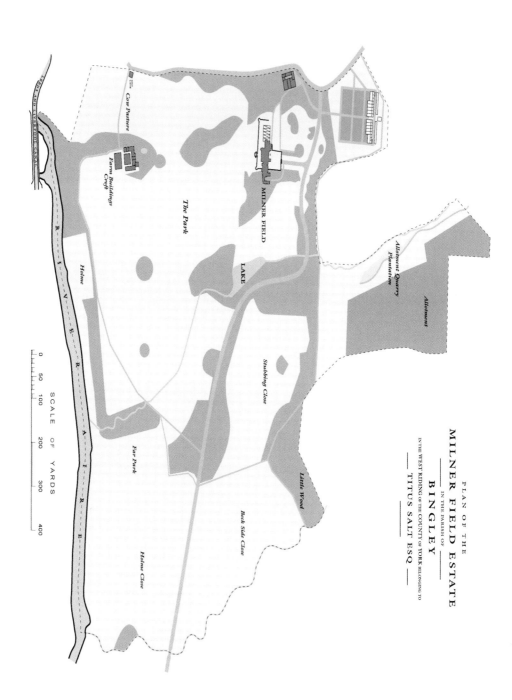

Fig 175: Plan of Milner Field estate.

PLAN OF THE
MILNER FIELD ESTATE
IN THE PARISH OF
BINGLEY
IN THE WEST RIDING OF THE COUNTY OF YORK BELONGING TO
TITUS SALT ESQ

SCALE OF YARDS
0   50   100   200   300   400

118

Appendices

285

Milner Field

1922

Milner Field
Estate

MILNER FIELD ESTATE
SALTAIRE, YORKSHIRE

Plans, Particulars & Conditions of Sale

.... of the above Estate comprising ....

FREEHOLD RESIDENTIAL
MANSION AND GROUNDS

FARMS, WOODLANDS,
BUILDING SITES, &c.

CONTAINING APPROXIMATELY
THREE HUNDRED ACRES

WILL BE OFFERED FOR SALE BY PUBLIC AUCTION
AT THE GREAT NORTHERN VICTORIA HOTEL
BRIDGE STREET, BRADFORD

On Thursday, 12th *October,* 1922, *at* 3-30 *p.m.*

BY

A. GADIE & SON

Auctioneers and Valuers

6 & 7 Thorpe Chambers, Bradford

::

SURVEYOR :
WM. ILLINGWORTH
15 Sunbridge Road, Bradford

SOLICITORS :
GAUNT, FOSTER & CO.
1 Cheapside, Bradford

Milner Field—
    General View
    Approach from Main Drive

123

Milner Field—
The Terrace View
Main Hall

LOT 1. *Coloured Pink on the Plan.*

Well adapted substantial Residence

known as

MILNER FIELD

built upon a commanding eminence overlooking the beautiful Valley of the River Aire. It is a self-contained and easily managed modern structure, with large Conservatory, Winter Gardens, Greenhouses, well-stocked Gardens, commodious Stables and Garages, two Entrances, Lodges, Woodlands, Grass Lands, Lake, etc. The position is ideal—woodland, park, river, lake, moor and meadow enrich its situation, and extensive bracing moorlands are within a few minutes.

The Mansion, which occupies a commanding position overlooking Airedale, was erected from the plans of Mr. Norman Shaw. It possesses its own water supply drawn from natural springs, its own filter beds, water-cooled dairies and storage rooms. Hunters' stabling, including automatic fodder hoist, good drains, and electric lighting.

The interior decorations of the Mansion are carried out in magnificent panelling of oak, teakwood, mahogany, chestnut, and cederwood.

THE MANSION CONTAINS:

ON THE GROUND FLOOR—Entrance Hall with Three-manual Organ, cloak room, lavatory and separate w.c., and housemaid's pantry ; Main Staircase, Drawing Room, Inner Hall giving exit to grounds, Dining Room, Library, Billiard Room, Lavatory, etc., with room adjoining fit up as private workshop; Office, Butler's Pantry, Servery, Butler's Private Room, large Conservatory or Winter Gardens, Kitchen, Scullery, two Larders, Butlery, Wash-house, Drying-room, Boiler-house, Coalplaces.

ON THE FIRST FLOOR—nine Bedrooms, three Dressing-rooms with Baths, Boudoir, Bathroom, three w.c.'s, Linen-room, Box-room.

ON THE SECOND FLOOR—numerous Bedrooms, Bathrooms, etc., for staff.

IN THE BASEMENT—Servants' Hall, and usual Offices.

There are Lodges, one at each end of the carriage drive. The one on the drive approached from Saltaire contains—Entrance Porch, Sitting Room, Kitchen, Larder, Store, Coalplace and w.c. approached from outside,—Bedrooms.

In the Conservatory, which, with the Winter Gardens, enclose about 500 square yards, are semi-tropical plants and exotics.

Fire pumps and appliances for obtaining water at high pressure in case of emergency, are to be found in the Conservatory.

In the Hall is a three-manual Organ built by Brindley & Foster, of Sheffield, in the year 1876. Its power is hydraulic and manual.

There are numerous Lawns, well-planted Gardens, Rosebeds, and Woodlands.

Milner Field has been the temporary home of the late King Edward, and in its grounds are trees which he planted. Our late Monarch and Queen Alexandra, when Prince and Princess of Wales, resided here as the guests of Mr. and Mrs. Salt in 1882. In May, 1887, Princess Beatrice and her husband, Prince Henry of Battenberg, also stayed at Milner Field.

SCHEDULE.

No. on Ordnance Plan	Cultivation	Area	
1244 (part of)	House, grounds and woodland	20·018	Township of Bingley
1245	Grass	3·258	do.
1246	Fish pond	·534	do.
1251 (part of)	Gardens	4·056	do.
1393	Grass	9·002	do.
1395	Woodland	1·307	do.
1396	Lodge and grounds	1·765	do.
1397 (part of)	Grass	5·220	do.
		45·160 acres.	

> **VACANT POSSESSION** of the whole of this Lot can be given on completion.

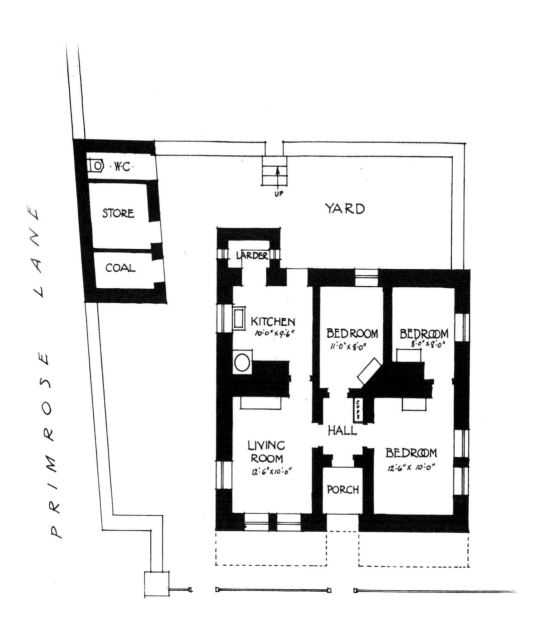

P R I M R O S E   L A N E

· W·C ·

STORE

COAL

UP

YARD

LARDER

KITCHEN
10′·0″ x 9′·6″

BEDROOM
11′·0″ x 8′·0″

BEDROOM
8′·0″ x 8′·0″

LIVING
ROOM
12′·6″ x 10′·0″

HALL

BEDROOM
12′·6″ x 10′·0″

PORCH

Ground Floor Plan of
Lodge at Eastern
Entrance to Lot 1.

CART   ROAD

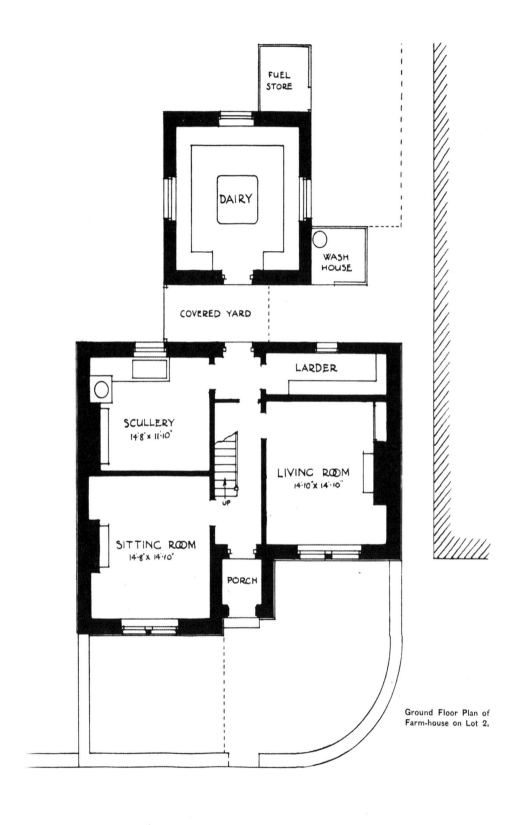

FUEL STORE

DAIRY

WASH HOUSE

COVERED YARD

LARDER

SCULLERY
14·8" x 11·10"

LIVING ROOM
14·10" x 14·10"

UP

SITTING ROOM
14·8" x 14·10"

PORCH

Ground Floor Plan of
Farm-house on Lot 2.

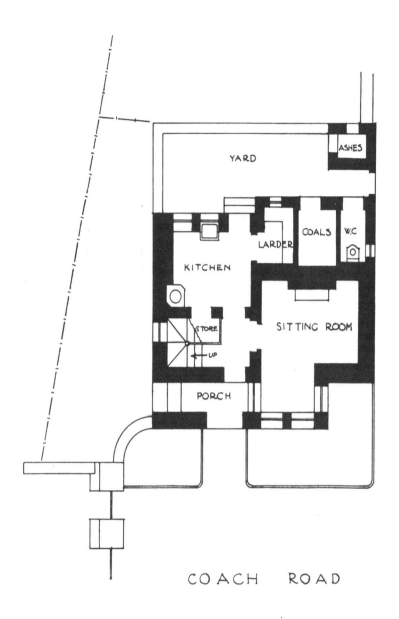

YARD

ASHES

LARDER

COALS

W.C

KITCHEN

SITTING ROOM

STORE

UP

PORCH

COACH ROAD

Ground Floor Plan of Residence at Western Entrance to Lot 2.

LOT 2. *Coloured Green on the Plan.*

The compact and choice Estate, comprising House and Farm Buildings and Land,

known as

MILNER FIELD FARM,

also a DETACHED RESIDENCE near the main road at Primrose Hill, with good land ripe for development, with frontage to River Aire and Primrose Lane.

Both Farm House, Farm Buildings, and the Detached Residence are substantially built and well adapted with Sheds, Stables, Mistals, Cow Byres, Fattening Byres, Barns, Granery, Cart Sheds, Open Sheds, Poultry Houses, etc.

DETACHED RESIDENCE CONTAINS:

ON THE GROUND FLOOR—Entrance Porch, Staircase Hall, Sitting room, Kitchen, Scullery, Larder, Dairy, Wash-house, Fuel Store.

ON THE FIRST FLOOR—three Bedrooms, one Box-room.

Numerous well-built Farm Buildings.

SCHEDULE.

No. on Ordnance Plan	Cultivation	Area	
689	Arable	·300	Township of Baildon
1179	Grass	2·778	Township of Bingley
1180	River Aire	2·758	do.
1181	Footpath and River bank	·995	do.
1182	Grass	1·745	do.
1183	Woodland	6·225	do.
1184	Grass	19·348	do.
1185	Farm house and grounds	2·485	do.
1186	Grass	5·329	do.
1187	Lodge and grounds	·358	do.
1243	Grass	14·417	do.
1244 (part of)	Woodland	1·130	do.
1397 (part of)	Grass	3·720	do.
1398 (part of)	River Aire	·890	do.
1399 (part of)	Footpath and River bank	·340	do.
1400 (part of)	Grass	10·468	do.
1400 (part of)	Arable	4·990	do.
1401 (part of)	Coach road	·270	do.

78·546 acres.

LOT 3. *Coloured Purple on the Plan.*

VALUABLE BUILDING LAND

on portion of Estate known as THE TOP GLEN, which can be economically cut into fourteen or more plots reserving a portion of the Woodland to each lot, or would be an ideal plot for anyone wanting to carry on a Fruit Farm or Poultry Farm.

SCHEDULE.

No. on Ordnance Plan	Cultivation	Area	
1247 (part of)	Woodland	6·433	Township of Bingley
1250 (part of)	Sparable Lane	·094	do.
1343 (part of)	Grass	5·168	do.
		11·695 acres.	

LOT 4. *Coloured Yellow on the Plan.*

VALUABLE BUILDING LAND

available for division into 17 plots.

SCHEDULE.

No. on Ordnance Plan	Cultivation	Area	
1346 (part of)	Footpath	·040	Township of Bingley
1391	Woodland	2·558	do.
1401 (part of)	Footpath	·080	do.
1402 (part of)	Grass	4·259	do.
1403 (part of)	Footpath	·165	do.
		7·102 acres.	

LOT 5. *Coloured Blue on the Plan.*

VALUABLE BUILDING LAND

available for division into 16 plots.

SCHEDULE.

No. on Ordnance Plan	Cultivation	Area	
1401 (part of)	Coach road and Footpath	·218	Township of Bingley
1402 (part of)	Grass	4·172	do.
		4·390 acres.	

Milner Field—
    Billiard Room
    The Conservatory

Milner Field—
A Lodge
A Lodge

LOT 6. *Coloured Green on the Plan.*

VALUABLE BUILDING LAND

available for division into 11 plots.

SCHEDULE.

No. on Ordnance Plan	Cultivation	Area	
627 (part of)	Woodland	5·098	Township of Baildon
627A(part of)	Footpath	·074	do.
627B(part of)	Woodland	1·609	do.
627C	do.	·033	do.
1402 (part of)	Grass	1·078	Township of Bingley
		7·892 acres.	

LOT 6A. *Coloured Blue on the Plan.*

VALUABLE WATER RIGHTS

WITH SITE OF RESERVOIR, ETC.

SCHEDULE.

No. on Ordnance Plan	Cultivation	Area	
573A	Reservoir	·136	Township of Baildon
627A (part of)	Footpath	·060	do.
1391A	Reservoir	·289	Township of Bingley
1403 (part of)	Footpath	·020	do.
		·505 acres.	

LOT 7. *Coloured Pink on the Plan.*

VALUABLE BUILDING LAND

available for division into 20 plots.

SCHEDULE.

No. on Ordnance Plan	Cultivation	Area	
627 (part of)	Woodland	2·118	Township of Baildon
627A(part of)	Footpath	·074	do.
627B(part of)	Woodland	1·009	do.
628 (part of)	Grass	2·510	do.
1402 (part of)	Grass	1·658	Township of Bingley
		7·369 acres.	

Lots 4, 5, 6, 6a & 7 will be first submitted in one lot, but if unsold will be offered as set out above.

LOT 8. *Coloured Yellow on the Plan.*

VALUABLE BUILDING LAND

available for division into 26 plots.

SCHEDULE.

No. on Ordnance Plan	Cultivation	Area	
628 (part of)	Grass	3·214	Township of Baildon
630A (part of)	Footpath	·010	do.
642 (part of)	Coach road	·060	do.
1401 (part of)	do.	·113	Township of Bingley
1402 (part of)	Grass	1·839	do.

5·236 acres.

LOT 9. *Coloured Purple on the Plan.*

VALUABLE BUILDING LAND

available for division into 25 plots.

SCHEDULE.

No. on Ordnance Plan	Cultivation	Area	
624 (part of)	Woodland	2·024	Township of Baildon
627 (part of)	do.	3·846	do.
627A (part of)	Footpath	·074	do.
627B (part of)	Woodland	·429	do.
628 (part of)	Grass	1·950	do.
630 (part of)	do.	·800	do.
630A (part of)	Footpath	·380	do.
632 (part of)	Grass	2·801	do.
634 (part of)	do.	·160	do.

12·464 acres.

LOT 10. *Coloured Pink on the Plan.*

VALUABLE BUILDING LAND

available for division into 8 or more plots.

SHOPS MAY BE ERECTED ON THIS SITE.

SCHEDULE.

No. on Ordnance Plan	Cultivation	Area	
628 (part of)	Grass	·050	Township of Baildon
629A (part of)	Footpath	·120	do.
630 (part of)	Grass	·454	do.
630A (part of)	Footpath	·030	do.
631 (part of)	Nursery	·260	do.
642 (part of)	Coach road	·260	do.
687 (part of)	Arable	2·350	do.

3·524 acres.

Lots 8, 9 & 10 will be first submitted in one lot, but if unsold will be offered as above.

LOT 11. *Coloured Green on the Plan.*

VALUABLE BUILDING LAND
available for division into 41 plots.

SCHEDULE.

No. on Ordnance Plan	Cultivation	Area	
624 (part of)	Woodland	4·458	Township of Baildon
634 (part of)	Grass	1·160	do.
635 (part of)	do.	1·090	do.
636 (part of)	do.	·403	do.
637 (part of)	do.	1·314	do.
638 (part of)	do.	1·720	do.
642 (part of)	do.	·260	do.
685 (part of)	Arable	·360	do.

10·765 acres.

LOT 12. *Coloured Yellow on the Plan.*

VALUABLE BUILDING LAND
available for division into 38 plots.

SCHEDULE.

No. on Ordnance Plan	Cultivation	Area	
624 (part of)	Woodland	2·224	Township of Baildon
636 (part of)	Grass	·084	do.
637 (part of)	do.	·120	do.
638 (part of)	do.	3·925	do.
639 (part of)	do.	2·652	do.
640 (part of)	Arable	·350	do.
642 (part of)	Coach road	·230	do.

9·581 acres.

LOT 13. *Coloured Blue on the Plan.*

VALUABLE BUILDING LAND
available for division into 38 plots.

SCHEDULE.

No. on Ordnance Plan	Cultivation	Area	
636 (part of)	Grass	·776	Township of Baildon
682 (part of)	River Aire	·630	do.
683 (part of)	Arable	1·060	do.
684 (part of)	Grass	·715	do.
685 (part of)	Arable	2·741	do.
686 (part of)	Cart road	·183	do.
687 (part of)	Nursery	2·870	do.

8·975 acres.

LOT 14. *Coloured Pink on the Plan.*

VALUABLE BUILDING LAND

available for division into 37 plots.

SCHEDULE.

No. on Ordnance Plan	Cultivation	Area	
636 (part of)	Grass	·232	Township of Baildon
639 (part of)	do.	·010	do.
640 (part of)	Arable	4·012	do.
642 (part of)	Coach road	·080	do.
682 (part of)	River Aire	·480	do.
683 (part of)	Arable	3·323	do.
684 (part of)	Grass	·755	do.
		8·892 acres.	

Lots 11, 12, 13 & 14 will be first submitted in one lot, but if unsold will be offered as set out above.

LOT 15. *Coloured Purple on the Plan.*

VALUABLE BUILDING LAND

available for division into 6 plots,

each having a large area of well-wooded land.

SCHEDULE.

No. on Ordnance Plan	Cultivation	Area	
618 (part of)	Woodland	·090	Township of Baildon
619 (part of)	Grass	·110	do.
621 (part of)	Woodland	6·880	do.
		7·080 acres.	

LOT 16. *Coloured Green on the Plan.*

VALUABLE BUILDING LAND

available for division into 10 plots.

Well-wooded portion to each plot.

SCHEDULE.

No. on Ordnance Plan	Cultivation	Area	
615 (part of)	Woodland	4·265	Township of Baildon
615B (part of)	do.	·744	do.
617 (part of)	Grass	·581	do.
618 (part of)	do.	·808	do.
		6·398 acres.	

LOT 17. *Coloured Blue on the Plan.*

VALUABLE BUILDING LAND

available for division into 7 plots.

Well-wooded portion to each plot.

SCHEDULE.

No. on Ordnance Plan	Cultivation	Area	
614 (part of)	Grass	·327	Township of Baildon
615 (part of)	Woodland	4·184	do.
615A (part of)	do.	·352	do.
615B (part of)	do.	·153	do.
617 (part of)	Grass	·681	do.
		5·697 acres.	

LOT 18. *Coloured Yellow on the Plan.*

VALUABLE BUILDING LAND

available for division into 11 plots.

Well-wooded portion to each plot.

SCHEDULE.

No. on Ordnance Plan	Cultivation	Area	
613 (part of)	Grass	1·439	Township of Baildon
614 (part of)	do.	·747	do.
615 (part of)	do.	6·938	do.
615A (part of)	do.	·261	do.
		9·385 acres.	

Lots 15, 16, 17 & 18 will be first submitted in one lot, but if unsold will be offered as above.

LOT 19. *Coloured Yellow on the Plan.*

VALUABLE BUILDING LAND

Shops may be erected on this Site.

SCHEDULE.

No. on Ordnance Plan	Cultivation	Area	
617 (part of)	Grass	·041	Township of Baildon
618 (part of)	do.	1·596	do.
619 (part of)	do.	·860	do.
643 (part of)	do.	·030	do.
644 (part of)	do.	·450	do.
645 (part of)	Road	·101	do.
		3·078 acres.	

LOT 20. *Coloured Pink on the Plan*

VALUABLE BUILDING LAND

available for division into 21 plots.

SCHEDULE.

No. on Ordnance Plan	Cultivation	Area	
614 (part of)	Grass	·891	Township of Baildon
617 (part of)	do.	·671	do.
643 (part of)	Arable	·010	do.
644 (part of)	Grass	1·621	do.
645 (part of)	Road	·161	do.
646 (part of)	Arable	·670	do.
677 (part of)	Grass	·214	do.
		4·238 acres.	

LOT 21. *Coloured Green on the Plan.*

VALUABLE BUILDING LAND

available for division into 16 plots.

SCHEDULE.

No. on Ordnance Plan	Cultivation	Area	
613 (part of)	Grass	·093	Township of Baildon
614 (part of)	do.	1·483	do.
645 (part of)	Road	·121	do.
646 (part of)	Arable	·777	do.
648 (part of)	Grass	·120	do.
677 (part of)	do.	·826	do.
		3·420 acres	

LOT 22. *Coloured Blue on the Plan.*

HOUSE AND FARM BUILDINGS

SCHEDULE.

No. on Ordnance Plan	Cultivation	Area	
612 (part of)	Barn, etc.	·320	Township of Baildon
613 (part of)	Grass	·083	do.
645 (part of)	Road	·061	do.
		·464 acres.	

Lots 19, 20, 21 & 22 will be first submitted in one lot, but if unsold
will be offered as above.

...er Field—
    Farm, Lot 2
    Detached Residence, Lot 2

LOT 23. *Coloured Green on the Plan.*

VALUABLE BUILDING LAND

available for division into 14 plots.

SCHEDULE.

No. on Ordnance Plan	Cultivation	Area	
619 (part of)	Grass	·020	Township of Baildon
642 (part of)	Coach road	·160	do.
643 (part of)	Grass	·640	do.
643 (part of)	Arable	2·024	do.
644 (part of)	Grass	·085	do.
645 (part of)	Road	·041	do.
677 (part of)	Grass	1·264	do.
		4·234 acres.	

LOT 24. *Coloured Yellow on the Plan.*

VALUABLE BUILDING LAND

available for division into 12 plots.

SCHEDULE.

No. on Ordnance Plan	Cultivation	Area	
642 (part of)	Coach road	·160	Township of Baildon
676 (part of)	Arable	1·352	do.
677 (part of)	Grass	1·802	do.
		3·314 acres.	

LOT 25. *Coloured Blue on the Plan.*

VALUABLE BUILDING LAND

available for division into 22 plots.

SCHEDULE.

No. on Ordnance Plan	Cultivation	Area	
642 (part of)	Coach road	·210	Township of Baildon
674 (part of)	Arable	2·588	do.
676 (part of)	do.	1·806	do.
677 (part of)	Grass	·306	do.
		4·910 acres.	

Lots 23, 24 & 25 will be first submitted in one lot, but if unsold will be offered as above.

LOT 26.   *Coloured Purple on the Plan.*

VALUABLE BUILDING LAND

available for division into 7 plots.

SCHEDULE.

No. on Ordnance Plan	Cultivation	Area	
642 (part of)	Coach road	·240	Township of Baildon
678 (part of)	Grass	2·670	do.
682 (part of)	River Aire	·340	do.
		3·250	

LOT 27.   *Coloured Green on the Plan.*

VALUABLE BUILDING LAND

available for division into 9 plots.

SCHEDULE.

No. on Ordnance Plan	Cultivation	Area	
642 (part of)	Coach road	·340	Township of Baildon
678 (part of)	Grass	3·060	do.
		3·400 acres.	

LOT 28.   *Coloured Pink on the Plan.*

VALUABLE BUILDING LAND

available for division into 10 plots.

SCHEDULE.

No. on Ordnance Plan	Cultivation	Area	
24 (part of)	Grass	2·972	Township of Baildon
642 (part of)	Coach road	·170	do.
682 (part of)	River Aire	·250	do.
		3·392 acres.	

Lots 26, 27 & 28 will be first submitted in one lot, but if unsold will be offered as above.

LOT 29. *Coloured Yellow on the Plan.*

VALUABLE BUILDING SITE

for Manufacturer's premises.

SCHEDULE.

No. on Ordnance Plan	Cultivation	Area	
14 (part of)	River Aire	·280	Township of Baildon
24 (part of)	Grass	3·902	do.
642 (part of)	Coach road	·400	do.
682 (part of)	River Aire	·360	do.
		4·942 acres.	

LOT 30. *Coloured Green on the Plan.*

VALUABLE BUILDING SITE

available for division into 16 plots.

SCHEDULE.

No. on Ordnance Plan	Cultivation	Area	
16 (part of)	Coach road	·040	Township of Baildon
22 (part of)	Grass	2·419	do.
642 (part of)	Coach road	·360	do.
674 (part of)	Arable	·437	do.
		3·256 acres.	

**Lots 29 and 30 will be first submitted in one lot, but if unsold
will be offered as above.**

GENERAL REMARKS.

The Estate has a river frontage of about two miles, and extends from Baildon
Bridge to Primrose Lane in the Bingley Area. The long drives through the Estate
are, of course, familiar to the many thousands of holiday-makers who make use of
them in order to reach the plateau at Shipley Glen. It is interesting to note in this
connection that there is a right of bridle-path along the main carriage drive (a section
of which is laid out with trees), a portion of the river side and other parts of the
Estate—a right of way for foot and horse, but not for vehicles.

The Estate as a whole has a southern aspect, is backed by beautiful woodlands, and is regarded as one of the finest building sites in the North of England.

The Midland Railway main lines is quite close ; also electric trams running between Bradford and Bingley and Bradford and Baildon Bridge are contiguous.

The Estate is known throughout the whole of the North of England, and even further afield, as a beauty spot, forming part of the country side known as Shipley Glen, and is easy of approach from all towns and cities in Yorkshire.

The purchaser of any lot will not be bound to adhere to the divisions shewn on the plan.

SUMMARY.

Lot 1	...	45·160 acres	Lot 17	...	5·697 acres
,, 2	...	78·546 ,,	,, 18	...	9·385 ,,
,, 3	...	11·695 ,,	,, 19	...	3·078 ,,
,, 4	...	7·102 ,,	,, 20	...	4·238 ,,
,, 5	...	4·390 ,,	,, 21	...	3·420 ,,
,, 6	...	7·892 ,,	,, 22	...	·464 ,,
,, 6A	...	·505 ,,	,, 23	...	4·234 ,,
,, 7	...	7·369 ,,	,, 24	...	3·314 ,,
,, 8	...	5·236 ,,	,, 25	...	4·910 ,,
,, 9	...	12·464 ,,	,, 26	...	3·250 ,,
,, 10	...	3·524 ,,	,, 27	...	3·400 ,,
,, 11	...	10·765 ,,	,, 28	...	3·392 ,,
,, 12	...	9·581 ,,	,, 29	...	4·942 ,,
,, 13	...	8·975 ,,	,, 30	...	3·256 ,,
,, 14	...	8·892 ,,			
,, 15	...	7·080 ,,	TOTAL		292·554 acres
,, 16	...	6·398 ,,			

SPECIAL CONDITIONS OF SALE

1. The General Conditions of the Yorkshire Union of Law Societies, a copy whereof can be inspected at the Offices of the Vendors' Solicitors at any time, shall be deemed to be incorporated with these Conditions, and these Conditions and the said General Conditions as aforesaid shall be construed together as one document, but if there be any inconsistency between them, these Conditions shall prevail.

2. In the General Conditions the Vendors' Solicitor means Messrs. Gaunt, Foster & Co., whose offices are situate at 1 Cheapside, Bradford.

3. In the General Conditions the Auctioneer means Messrs. A. Gadie & Son, of 6 and 7 Thorpe Chambers, Hustlergate, Bradford.

4. The deposit shall be at the rate of 10 per cent. on the purchase money.

5. The Abstract of Title shall be delivered or sent through the general post to the Purchaser or his Solicitor within ten days after the date of Sale, together with a copy of the Special Conditions and of the Sale Plan so far as applicable.

6. The Title shall commence as to Lots 1, 2, 3, 4, 5, and parts of Lots 6, 6A, 7 and 8, with an Indenture dated the 8th day of April, 1903, and made between Catherine Salt of the one part, and James Roberts of the other part; and as to the remaining lots, with an Indenture dated the 6th day of October, 1919, and made between Sir Shirley Harris Salt and Harold Crossley Salt of the first part, Sir Titus Salt, Bart., Sons & Company Limited of the second part, and Sir James Roberts of the third part. With regard to this latter deed it may be pointed out that Sir James Roberts agreed to purchase the property comprised in the last mentioned Indenture many years ago (and not recently as stated in the Indenture), and entered into possession, and so continued to the date of the agreement with the Vendors hereinafter mentioned, but the actual conveyance was only taken to Sir James Roberts upon the date appearing in the said Indenture. The plan attached to this Indenture is apparently not the plan intended to be attached, and consequently some discrepancy arises between the descriptions in the Indenture and the colourings shewn upon the plan. A plan will be produced shewing the correct colourings for the purpose of identification with the description in the Indenture, and each purchaser shall assume, as is the fact, that the said Sir James Roberts became by virtue of the said Indenture the owner in fee simple free from incumbrances of all the properties shewn upon the last mentioned plan.

7. The present Vendors purchased some time ago from Sir James Roberts the properties comprised in the particulars hereinbefore set forth, but no Conveyance thereof has yet been executed to them, and the Vendors will procure for each Purchaser an effective Conveyance executed by all necessary parties; and no Purchaser shall be entitled to call for the Agreement for Sale between Sir James Roberts and the Vendors.

8. Objections to and requisitions on the Title shall be delivered within ten days from the delivery of the Abstract, whether the Abstract shall be delivered within the above time or not, and all further objections and requisitions arising out of the replies to any former objections and requisitions shall be delivered within four days from the receipt of such replies.

9. The tenure of the property is Freehold.

10. The purchase shall be completed at the offices of the Vendors' Solicitors on the 9th day of November, 1922. In case any Purchaser shall desire to defer completion of his purchase, such purchase may be postponed until the 31st day of December, 1923, and such Purchaser shall be given immediate possession of his purchase (subject to any existing tenancy) he paying interest on the balance of his purchase money at the rate of 5 per cent. per annum until completion.

11. The draft assurance shall be sent to the Vendors' Solicitors ten days, and the approved draft and engrossment seven days before the date fixed for completion.

12. The property is sold subject to all rights of way, light, drainage or other easements affecting the same, and in particular to all easements of water pipes acquired by the Bradford Corporation or the Shipley District Council, or any other authority of the like kind, and also to the provisions of any town planning scheme or other scheme under the Town Planning Acts or any other Acts of a similar nature.

13. Each Purchaser shall have general rights of way at all times and for all purposes in common with the Vendors and all other persons to whom they have already granted or may hereafter grant similar rights, and so far as the Vendors shall have power to grant the same, to and from the plot of land purchased by him over and along the whole of any intended streets or roads shewn on the Sale Plan as and when such intended streets or roads shall be made, and not previously, and also the use in common as aforesaid of any sewers made or intended to be made under the said intended streets or roads. Until any such streets or roads are formed, each Purchaser shall be afforded such rights of way as may be necessary and convenient for the purpose of access to and from the said plot of land purchased by him, from and to the nearest road belonging to the Vendors which shall at present be in existence.

14. The Vendors reserve to themselves, their heirs, executors, administrators and assigns, general rights of way at all times and for all purposes in common with each Purchaser and all other persons entitled to similar rights over and along such part or parts of the plot of land purchased as are to be appropriated by the Purchaser towards the said streets or roads as shewn upon the Sale Plan in pursuance of the provisions hereinafter contained, and also the right to lay down and to renew and repair gas and water pipes, and electric or other cables under any part of the said intended streets or roads, and also the use of any drains or sewers to be constructed under the said intended streets or roads, with liberty to enter into and upon the plot of land purchased for the purpose of laying, renewing or repairing the said drains, gas and water pipes and cables, and of constructing, opening, cleansing or repairing the said sewers or making connections therewith. And the Vendors also reserve the right to grant unto any person or persons whomsoever such rights of way and drainage, and the right to lay down, renew and repair pipes and cables, as aforesaid.

15. Each Purchaser shall forthwith at his own expense appropriate from the plot of land purchased and for ever leave open unbuilt upon and unobstructed the portion or portions thereof coloured brown upon the Sale Plan within the boundary lines of the plot of land purchased towards the said intended streets or roads, and shall at the like expense, and according to the directions of the Vendors or their Surveyor or Agent, if and when required so to do, forthwith form, make, drain and channel the portions of the said streets or roads included in his purchase in such manner, of such materials and dimensions, and of such widths as to the causeway and carriage way as shall be specified by the Vendors or their Surveyor or Agent aforesaid, and shall also construct under the same portion or portions of the said intended streets or roads, main drains or sewers of such material and dimensions as shall be required by the Vendors or their Surveyor or Agent. And also shall, if and when called upon so to do, pave, flag or macadam the same portion of the said streets or roads in accordance with the directions of the Vendors or their Surveyor or Agent, and shall keep the same portions of streets or roads and the sewers thereunder in a good and satisfactory state of repair and condition, until the same shall be taken over by the local authority.

16. Notwithstanding the foregoing provisions the Vendors may if they shall think fit, and if not already done, make, form and complete the said streets or roads shewn upon the Sale Plan, and pave and flag the same, and construct the sewers thereunder in such manner, of such materials and of such dimensions as to the said sewers, and at such time or times as they may think expedient; and power is hereby expressly reserved to the Vendors to do such work, and for that purpose to enter upon each plot of land purchased; and each Purchaser shall on demand pay to the Vendors a fair proportion of the expenses of and incident to such work, whether already done or hereafter to be done, which proportion shall be fixed by the Vendors' Surveyor, whose decision shall be final, and the amount thereof shall be a first charge upon the said plot of land, and shall carry interest at the rate of 5 per cent. per annum from the date when demand for payment shall be made until payment thereof.

17. No Purchaser shall encroach upon the causeways of the said streets or roads.

18. No window lights or openings shall be put out in any building or wall which may be erected upon any plot of land purchased so as to look or open immediately upon the adjoining land of the Vendors within a distance of ten yards thereof without the previous consent in writing of the Vendors.

19. Each Purchaser shall forthwith at his own expense erect and for ever maintain in good repair a good and substantial wall or fence of a height of not less than $4\frac{1}{2}$ feet along each side of the plot of land purchased by him which adjoins upon other property of the Vendors.

20. The Purchaser of each lot having a frontage to the River Aire shall have full rights of way, so far as the Vendors can lawfully grant the same, over the whole of the River Aire co-extensive with the remaining land belonging to the Vendors, in common with the Vendors and all other persons already having or to whom the Vendors may hereafter grant similar rights. And the Vendors reserve to themselves full rights of way and other water rights over and under the portion of the said river included in the plot purchased.

21. Each Purchaser of any plot having a frontage to the said river shall not at any time do or suffer, or permit to be done, anything which shall in any way pollute or prejudice the water of the said river, or in any way impede or interfere with the flow of the said river as at present.

22. No buildings or erections shall, without the consent in writing of the Vendors, be erected upon any plots of land save and except the following :—

As to Lots 1 to 14 (except Lot 10) detached dwelling-houses with the usual outbuildings, garage and offices thereto of a not less constructional value, exclusive of the cost of the land, of £800, the site of each such dwelling-house to occupy not less than half an acre of land.

As to Lots 15 to 30 (except Lot 19) detached or semi-detached dwelling-houses with the usual outbuildings, garage and offices thereto of a constructional value of not less than £500 exclusive of the site.

As to Lots 10 and 19, detached or semi-detached dwelling-houses or shops, or dwelling-houses and shops, with the usual outbuildings, garage and out-offices thereto, of a not less constructional value than £800 exclusive of the site.

23. Plans of all buildings proposed to be erected upon any plot or plots purchased shall be first submitted to and approved by the Vendors' Surveyor.

24. No noisy, noxious or offensive trade or business, or any business which shall cause or be likely to cause any nuisance, annoyance, danger or inconvenience to the Vendors or to the owners or occupiers for the time being of any adjoining land, shall be carried on upon any part of the estate.

25. No hoardings of any description, nor any conspicuous advertisements or other signs, shall be erected or exhibited upon any part of the estate.

26. All growing timber, plantations and underwood are included in the sale, but no purchaser shall cut down any timber upon any lot purchased by him save such as may be necessary for the benefit of the remaining timber standing upon such plot, or to form such clearing as, in the opinion of the Vendors or their Surveyor, may be necessary for the building of a dwelling-house or the formation of a suitable garden thereto, it being the intention of the Vendors, so far as may be necessary for preserving the natural beauty of the estate, to retain all ornamental timber now standing and growing upon the estate; but this provision shall not in any way be deemed to preclude the Vendors from dealing with such woodland or any part thereof in any manner as to them may seem fit.

27. The sale shall not include any growing crops standing upon any land purchased at the date of sale, and the right is reserved to the Vendors and their tenants to enter upon each plot purchased and to remove, within such period of time as may be reasonably required, all such growing crops.

28. The property is sold subject to all tenant's or customary rights, and each purchaser shall be liable to any tenant thereof for any compensation due to such tenant under the Agricultural Holdings Acts or any other similar Act for the time being in force.

29. The Vendors reserve such rights under and over the land under which are situate the water pipes running from the Reservoir shewn on the said plan to the River Aire, and within a distance of five yards from each side of the said pipes as may be necessary for the full use and enjoyment of the said pipes, and for the conveyance of water from the said Reservoir to the said River or to any other point to which the Vendors may desire to have such water conveyed, with the right to enter upon such portion of land at any time for the purpose of inspecting, renewing, relaying or repairing the said pipes, or for any other purposes in connection therewith.

30. The Vendors reserve the right at any time hereafter to lay down a sewer along the portions of land lying adjacent to the River Aire, or in such other position as may be found necessary or convenient for the proper and effective drainage of any part of the estate, and the right to enter upon any portion of the land sold for the purpose of constructing, opening, cleansing or repairing the said sewer, doing as little damage as may be, and making good the surface of the land, and no purchaser shall be entitled to any compensation for any disturbance or interference arising out of the construction or maintenance of any such sewer.

31. The property is sold subject to all existing leases and tenancy agreements affecting the same, and in particular (as to Lot 6A) to an Indenture of Lease bearing date the 15th day of December, 1919, and made between Sir James Roberts, Baronet, of the one part, and Sir Titus Salt, Bart., Sons & Co. Ltd., of the other part, being a lease of the water rights from the Reservoir of the estate for a period of ten years from the 1st day of February, 1918, at an annual rental of £500 upon the terms and conditions therein contained.

32. Each Purchaser shall have rights of way and traffic (for vehicles not exceeding 2½ tons) over the Bridge leading from Saltaire to the entrance to the estate over the River Aire, and shall be liable to a proportionate part of any expenses hereafter incurred in the maintenance and painting of the said bridge until such time as the said bridge shall be taken over by any local authority, such proportionate part to be based upon the proportion which the area of any lot acquired by each purchaser shall bear to the total estate comprised in these particulars.

33. The Vendors reserve the right to themselves, their nominees, and their successors in title, to alter the line or direction of any street or road in any portion of the estate remaining unsold, notwithstanding the foregoing provisions, and to connect any sewer or drain which they may cause to be constructed in connection with any such land or the buildings thereon with any sewer or drain which may be constructed under the provisions herein contained and, if necessary, to alter or enlarge the same without payment for so doing and generally to vary the lay-out aud development scheme as shewn upon the plan annexed to these particulars in such manner as they or their Surveyor or Agent may from time to time think fit, and nothing herein contained shall be deemed to bind the Vendors to carry out or complete any lay-out scheme as shewn upon the said plan or preclude them from afterwards selling any portion of the said estate for the time being unsold upon such terms and conditions as they may think fit.

34. A Plan of each Lot purchased shall be prepared by the Vendors' Surveyor at the expense of the Purchaser, and shall at the like expense be endorsed on the Conveyance to the Purchaser.

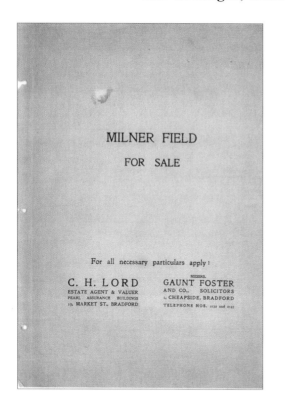

MILNER FIELD

FOR SALE

For all necessary particulars apply :

C. H. LORD
ESTATE AGENT & VALUER.
PEARL ASSURANCE BUILDINGS,
19, MARKET ST., BRADFORD.

MESSRS.
GAUNT FOSTER
AND CO.,   SOLICITORS
1, CHEAPSIDE, BRADFORD
TELEPHONE NOS. 2134 and 2135

MILNER FIELD ESTATE

MILNER FIELD is a beautiful modern residence built upon a commanding eminence, overlooking its own surrounding estates and possessing delightful views over the greater part of the Valley of the Aire. Its position is such that woodland and park, lake and river, hillside, moor and meadow, enrich its situation with their varied charms, to the total exclusion of all other scenes.

All that is beautiful in nature, combined with all that is well planned of man, helps the Milner Field Estate to keep its proud position in the niche occupied by the stately structures of the West Riding. There is nothing common or mean about its bold and pleasing outline; nothing but the finest which craftsmanship could produce was used in its erection.

Essentially a modern structure, Milner Field is probably the most self-contained and self-managed house in Yorkshire—it is certainly one of the richest in interior decorations and appointments.

From the house's proximity to that flourishing little town of mushroom growth, Saltaire, one might be tempted to think that a vista of mill chimneys and dreary buildings would be the only outlook from its terraces and windows. However, such is not the case. Milner Field is unique in its choice of position, a testimony to the care its builders and late owners took to ensure the complete blotting out of all harsh objects appertaining to the work-a-day world.

Erected from the plans of that eminent architect, Mr. Norman Shaw, by the late Sir Titus Salt, the house is complete in every detail. Amongst its appurtenances which tend to guarantee the maximum of comfort for its possessor, Milner Field boasts its own water supplies, drawn

from natural and never-failing springs, its own filter beds, elaborate electric lighting and telephonic communication systems, water cooled dairies and storage rooms, whilst even the provision for hunters' stabling is an outstanding testimony to the house's perfect equipment, including, as it does, automatic fodder hoists, good drains and electric lighting.

The decorative work of the house at once chaste and magnificently appointed, is carried out in panellings of oak, teakwood, mahogany, chestnut and cedarwood, and elaborate devices of carving, some of them executed in timbers of the 15th century, are features showing the taste of Milner Field's first owners.

Its Winter Gardens and conservatory an enclosure of some 500 square yards, is lofty, well heated and arranged upon the grand style. The semi-tropical plants and exotics, which cluster about the marble statuary within its interior, lend an air of almost princely magnificence to the surroundings. The floor of this huge glass-enclosed structure is harmonious with many of the other Italian evidences of architecture in the composite whole of Milner Field. It is of carefully designed mosaic work copying the famous Mosaic of the Roman Pavements and villa floors. Two marble statues, original works of some considerable worth, are erected within the conservatory.

Fire pumps and appliances for obtaining water at high pressure, in case of emergency, are to be found in the conservatory and are among the evidences of perfect equipment and forethought on the part of the builders.

In the hall of Milner Field is a three-manual Organ built by Messrs. Brindley & Foster of Sheffield in the year 1876 to the order of the Salt Family; its power is hydraulic and manual. This instrument seems to have been mellowed and improved by age, for, after some recent and very exhaustive tests, two experts upon organ construction and instrumentality pronounced a verdict that its "voicing" was one of the most resonant and perfect that they had heard. Again that adherence to detail which so embellishes and enriches the house of Milner Field; the many little appliances on and near the organ which make for easy organist's work could only be adequately described by an instrument builder or an organ enthusiast.

Milner Field has been the temporary home of the late King Edward, and in its ground are trees which he planted; his study lies in one of the sunniest apartments of the residence.

Our late Monarch and Queen Alexandra when they were Prince and Princess of Wales, resided at Milner Field as guests of Mr. and Mrs. Salt, upon the occasion of the opening of the Bradford Technical College in the year 1882. Five years later, in May, 1887, Princess Beatrice and her husband, Prince Henry of Battenberg, stayed at Milner Field before the opening ceremony which they performed at the Royal Yorkshire Jubilee Exhibition held at Saltaire.

This residence has housed many men and women of distinction and, as a fitting abode for Royalty, Milner Field has proved its worth among the stately homes of the West Riding.

It is not known exactly when the first house was built at Milner Field, but one is safe in assuming that the two great families of Milner and Oldfield possessed manorial lands in this district—circa A.D. 1400-53.

There are sufficient authentic records in existence to prove that in the reign of Queen Elizabeth the dilapidated Hall of the first-named family was re-built, renovated and extended by the heirs of the Oldfield family, to whom it passed in line of marriage. The house, which was displaced by the present edifice, retained many of the characteristics of the Elizabethan period in architecture; two carved armorial devices and the interlaced monograms, "I.O." "M.O." (the initials of the head of the family and his wife), were located above the hall doorway. Surmounting the Dower-house doorway on the Milner Field Estate these initials are to be seen carved on a stone slab, and a date, 1603, testifies to the family's long tenancy of these possessions.

Two gateposts of the Elizabethan period, imposing and well preserved, stand on the old-world terraces which are situated near the modern house.

Out of the possession of the Oldfields the residence passed into the Fells' possession (an old Bingley family) and next to the Rev. Mr. Penny by marriage. In the year 1844 Mr. Penny sold Milner Field to Mr. John Wilmer Field, of Heaton Hall, Shipley, who, dying shortly afterwards, left his two daughters co-heiresses of his possessions. One of these ladies married Lord Oxmantown (afterwards Earl Rosse), and carried into that family the extensive Shipley Estates; the other daughter of Mr. J. Wilmer Field married Admiral Duncombe; and it was from her representatives that Mr. Salt acquired the Milner Field manorial lands in 1869. A Mr. Harris, of London, was engaged by the new owner, and was given the task of dismantling the old residence and erecting the present structure.

After passing along the North side of the park of some 150 acres the Hall is reached through a court-yard, at the entrance of which stands an elegant ivy-covered archway. All around is a wealth of lawns and woodlands, flowers and gardens, shrubbery and rosebeds. There is also a large lake and fishpond spanned in one narrow part by a rustic bridge; a good boathouse is erected on the shore of the lake and there are two or three pleasure skiffs.

The stabling and kitchen gardens of the residence are on the Primrose Lane side of the grounds, where there is an entrance with a lodge, one of four distinctively designed houses serving this purpose to the Estate.

Milner Field, with its two miles sweep of the river, its magnificent views (in some directions one can see a distance of 30 miles over the rolling moorlands) and its lordly setting in picturesque and natural surroundings, is a country gentleman's house *par excellence* and will, no doubt, prove a fitting residence for some gentleman who loves the grand in nature as much as he appreciates the surroundings of comfort and the evidences of taste which can be found in such a distinctive residence and Estate as Milner Field.

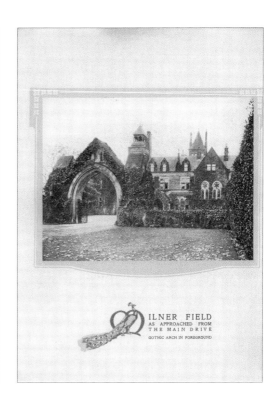

MILNER FIELD
AS APPROACHED FROM
THE MAIN DRIVE
GOTHIC ARCH IN FOREGROUND

MILNER FIELD
SHOWING STYLE OF
ARCHITECTURE
AND CLOCK TOWER

THE VINERIES

THE GREENHOUSES

AGE.
OLD GATEWAY REMAINING FROM
THE FORMER MANOR HOUSE OF THE
OLDFIELD FAMILY, BUILT UPON THE
SITE NOW OCCUPIED BY MILNER FIELD

LIGHT OVER SURFACE
OF THE QUIET LAKE

AN UNUSUAL
TYPE OF LODGE

THE STABLES

MILNER FIELD'S
KITCHEN

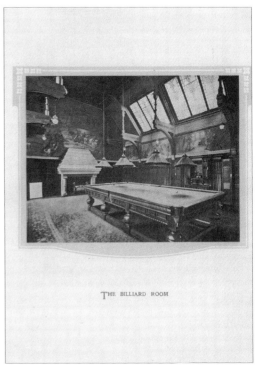

THE BILLIARD ROOM

T WO FARMS ON
MILNER FIELD ESTATE

M ILNER FIELD VIEWED
FROM THE LAWNS

O NE OF THE PICTU-
RESQUE LODGES

T ERRACE VIEW
MILNER FIELD

T HE CONSERVATORY
THERE ARE OVER 90 SQUARE
YARDS UNDER GLASS

A RECEPTION ROOM

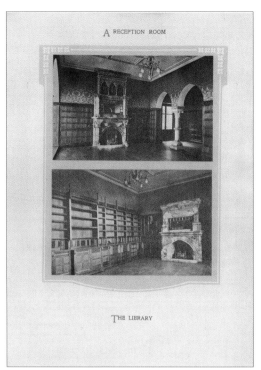

THE LIBRARY

A TERRACE VIEW OF MILNER FIELD SHOWING CONSERVATORY

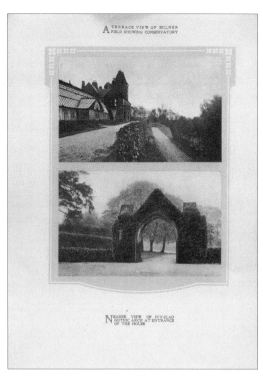

NEARER VIEW OF IVY-CLAD GOTHIC ARCH AT ENTRANCE OF THE HOUSE

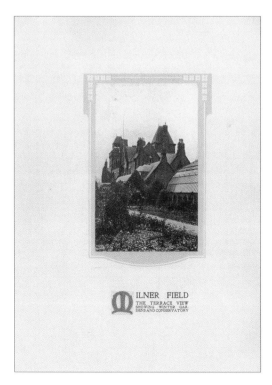

MILNER FIELD
THE TERRACE VIEW SHOWING WINTER GARDENS AND CONSERVATORY

THE DINING ROOM

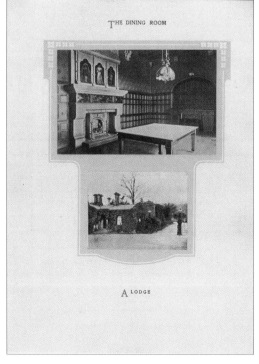

A LODGE

T HE HALL OF THE HOUSE
SHOWING THE GREAT ORGAN AND
THE MAGNIFICENT OAK PANEL-
LINGS AND CARVINGS

A CORNER OF THE LAKE
IN THE GROUNDS

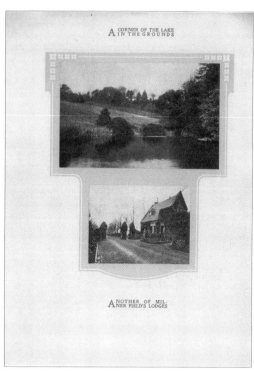

A NOTHER OF MIL-
NER FIELD'S LODGES

A BEAUTIFUL CORNER   T HE APPROACH TO
OF THE GROUNDS   THE CONSERVATORY

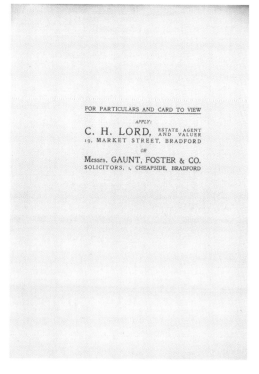

FOR PARTICULARS AND CARD TO VIEW

APPLY:

C. H. LORD, ESTATE AGENT
            AND VALUER
19, MARKET STREET, BRADFORD

OR

Messrs. GAUNT, FOSTER & CO.
SOLICITORS, 1, CHEAPSIDE, BRADFORD

155

The Knoll and Ferniehurst
by Letitia Lawson

THE KNOLL

From the mid nineteenth century onwards Baildon was beginning to change from a small community where people made a living principally by farming, quarrying, mining and textiles. Wealthy manufacturers began to build large houses in the Baildon area and, in so doing, helped to change Baildon into a suburb for Bradford and Leeds; a process which continues to this day.

The Salt family was among the first to plan to build a house in the Baildon area. The area was ideally placed for the family as it was located just across the river from Saltaire: the source of their fortune. In 1856 (Sir) Titus Salt bought a farmhouse and land situated at Baildon Green from the Ferrand family of Bingley for £3,000.

The farm was leased to the Fairbank family, who were farmers and clothiers and who had lived there for over one hundred years. The farmhouse, situated at the bottom of a wooded and rocky hill, had fine views across the valley towards Shipley and Saltaire.

It is possible that (Sir) Titus Salt had intended to build a house there for one of his sons, but for some reason he sold the land to Charles Stead for £3,400. Interestingly, Stead was the first man to be appointed a director at Salts mill who was not a member of the Salt family and he had been appointed a junior director of the firm in 1854.

It is thought that the proposed building of working class houses along what is now Green Lane could have been the reason for the sale or it may just have been that (Sir) Titus Salt preferred another site at Baildon.

Charles Stead, however, obviously felt the site had potential and in 1858 he submitted a building plan to the newly-formed Baildon Local Board for a house to be built on top of the wooded hill. This was the first building plan submitted to the Board and is briefly described as a plan for a house and buildings at the Knoll. This appears to be the first time the area was referred to as the Knoll.

The wooded area where the house was to be built had previously been known as Fairbanks Wood, however the Knoll does seem to be a better description of the rocky and wooded area. The plan was passed but unfortunately does not survive; indeed none of the early building plans for Baildon remain.

Later photographs do show the house was of gothic design, had a tower, was decorated with crenellations and gargoyles and was situated at the top of the hill and would have enjoyed magnificent views across the valley to Saltaire (Fig 187).

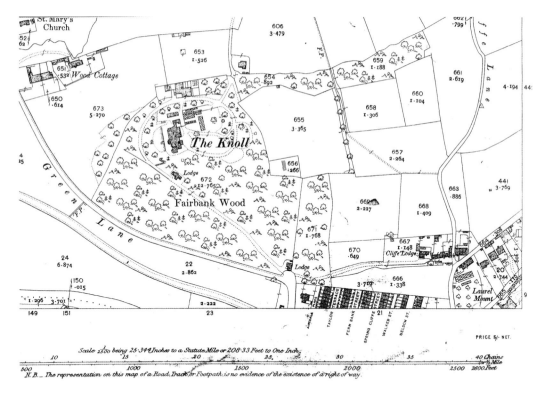

Fig 176: Early Ordnance Survey map detail of The Knoll.

Formal gardens were laid out in the grounds and more informal gardens were laid out on the hillside and round the drive that led down to two lodges, one of which still exists. There was also a kitchen garden tucked away in the upper corner of the woodland.

The farm was still rented out to the Fairbank family but, of course, the amount of land attached to it was now reduced. Eventually the Fairbank family moved to Windhill and the farmhouse was altered and made into two houses, one of which was known as Bank House.

Bank House was rented out to a Swiss businessman – one must presume that the increasing demand for houses in the more rural area around Bradford meant that it was more profitable to rent houses to businessmen than to tenant farmers.

The Stead family lived at the Knoll in some style; the 1881 census shows that they had a cook, maid, two housemaids, kitchen maid and also employed a Swiss governess/teacher as well as outdoor staff.

Unfortunately, this was not to last. Sir Titus Salt died in 1876 and in 1881 the firm became a limited liability company.

Charles Stead was mill manager and Titus Salt Jnr became company secretary. However, when Titus Salt Jnr died suddenly in 1887, his brother Edward was left as the only

Fig 177: Above: Brenda Armstrong at the Knoll in 1961.

Fig 178: Above: Detail of the underside of a bay window at the Knoll, circa 1961. (John Irwin)

Fig 179: Below. Aerial image of the Knoll in its thickly-wooded grounds.

Fig 180: Left. The Knoll, courtyard and entrance, during Brenda Armstrong's visit in 1961.

Fig 181: Below. The encroachment of modern housing estates on the former grounds of the Knoll can clearly be seen in this rare aerial image. The location of the recently demolished house is circled. Taken on 20th March 1963 (Reproduced courtesy of BKS Surveys Ltd). The Knoll Lodge, which still exists today, is also circled.

member of the Salt family on the board of directors. Charles Stead was elected the chairman of the board of directors and C.F. Stead became a director in place of Titus Jnr.

By the early 1890s the firm was facing serious financial problems. The American market was closed to imports of plush fabric in 1890 and so Salts opened a plush factory at Bridgeport, U.S.A. in an attempt to continue its business in plush weaving. Unfortunately the scheme failed, there were job losses in Saltaire and profits were reduced. In 1882 Charles Stead had mortgaged his house and grounds to the Bradford Banking Company as security for the firm and when, in 1893, the firm was wound-up (and eventually purchased by a syndicate of Bradford businessmen including James Roberts) the bank foreclosed on the mortgage and Stead lost the house.

He moved to Freshfield near Southport, where he died a few years later.

On 28th December 1893, the Bradford Banking Company sold the mansion house and grounds to James Roberts and his family for £10,000. According to the 1901 Census they too had a Swiss governess (Elizabeth Hohr from Zurich) together with a cook, two housemaids and a footman.

James Roberts eventually became managing director and chairman of Salts and in 1903 he purchased Milner Field from Titus Jnr's widow and also erected the statue of Sir Titus Salt in Saltaire Park.

When his eldest son, Bertram, was married in 1903 the employees were given a holiday and tea in the park.

In 1905 James Roberts conveyed the Knoll to Bertram who, in 1904, had become a joint managing director with his father. Unfortunately Bertram died young (as did two of his brothers) in January 1912 and the house, not unlike Milner Field in this regard, gained a reputation as being an unlucky house in which to live.

On 25th September 1919, Bertram's widow, Eliza Gertrude Roberts, sold the house and grounds to William Root for £10,500. A succession of owners followed and at one time a scheme was floated to turn the house into a museum.

Interestingly, on 29th April 1938 the *Telegraph & Argus* reported that a Baildon Councillor, John Kerr, had bought the mansion, farm buildings and fifty three acres of land at a cost of £6,700 and intended to demolish it and use the land for building purposes (he had already developed three estates in the Baildon area). It was said that he planned to erect more than six hundred houses on the site. No official records of this sale seem to remain and it could be that perhaps the sale was never finalised.

Records relating to the ownership of the property around this period are very confusing and would merit more detailed investigation. What is known is that William Root died and his

Fig: 182: Above. James Roberts in his Summer House.

Fig: 183: Above. Left to right. James William, Bertram, James Roberts, unknown, unknown.

Fig: 184. Above. Left to right. Unknown, unknown, Bertram, James Roberts standing in profile, James William, pose at the Knoll front door.

Fig: 185: Below. Governess, May, Alice, Harry Roberts.

Fig: 186: Below. Alice, Harry, Governess, May Roberts.

Fig: 187: Left to Right. Governess,Harry, Alice, May Roberts outside The Knoll.

executors sold the Knoll estate to William Denby Roberts, the solicitor son of Bertram, in 1938 and eventually (as a result of a compulsory purchase order) Baildon Council bought it for £8,950 on 31st January 1946. It would seem that the Council intended to develop the Baildon Green area and wanted to build on the estate, though they do not appear to have wanted to demolish the house.

At that time the house was described as unoccupied and the Council decided to convert it into flats, which were apparently used by Council officials. The Council opened the grounds as a pleasure ground for Baildon in around 1948 - Mrs Roberts attended and performed the opening - and a series of rules were devised for their use. No person was allowed to take any cattle, sheep, goats or pigs into the grounds, nor was one allowed to bathe in any ornamental lake or to pluck any bud, blossom or flower.

The house itself was pulled down around 1961 and council flats were built on the site. Fig 181 is a detailed aerial shot of the Knoll estate taken on 20th March 1963 and shows the site of the mansion has been cleared, though the topiary and formal gardens can still clearly be seen. The modern housing development that now occupies the area had not yet been built.

The lodge at the bottom of the carriage drive still survives as do the grounds; however they are rather overgrown and the drive is now really only used by dog walkers.

Bertram Roberts' connection with the house is commemorated in the name of nearby Bertram Drive.

FERNIEHURST

It was not until the early 1860s that a member of the Salt family finally built a house in Baildon.

In 1862 (Sir) Titus Salt conveyed land adjoining Baildon Road to his third son Edward who then proceeded to build what became known as Ferniehurst (possibly for his new wife). There is no mention of a building plan in the Baildon registers and unfortunately there are no known photographs of the house.

It is possible, however, to form an idea of what the house looked like from a sale catalogue that was prepared when the house was put up for auction in 1893. It is described as a mansion house with a drawing room, library, dining room, butler's pantry, twelve bedrooms, a tower, a billiard room which had a separate staircase and a large lavatory adjoining and the house also had accommodation for servants, including a servants' hall.

At the time of the 1871 census Edward Salt had a butler, housekeeper, housemaid, kitchen maid and even a pageboy as well as a coachman, gardeners and other staff. There were also two bathrooms, (one with WC) and two housemaids' rooms with WCs. The residence was efficiently heated by coils and piping from the greenhouse boiler.

Particulars.

THE

FERNIEHURST ESTATE

(Now occupied by Edward Salt, Esq.), comprising

THE MANSION HOUSE,

CONTAINING ON THE

BASEMENT—Wine and Beer Cellars.

GROUND FLOOR—Vestibule, Hall, Dining Room, Drawing Room, Library, Store Room, Cloak Room, Lavatory, w.c., Butler's Pantry, Kitchen, Housekeeper's Room, Servants' Hall, Business Room and two Larders.

FIRST FLOOR—Seven Bedrooms, Dressing Room fitted with bath, Two Bath Rooms (one with w.c.), Linen Room, and two Housemaids' Rooms with w.c.'s.

The Billiard Room (to which access is obtained by a separate stone staircase), with large lavatory adjoining.

SECOND FLOOR—Five Bedrooms and Man-servant's Room.

THE TOWER—Box Room.

OUTBUILDINGS of an extensive, complete, and useful character.

STABLING, at a convenient distance from the residence, and of a perfect description, comprising accommodation for ten horses, Carriage House for six carriages, Harness and Cleaning Rooms, Glass-covered Paved Yard, and Horses' Wash Box, with a Tan Ride for exercise adjoining.

A PICTURESQUE and Commodious Lodge at the entrance gates.

A MODEL FARM, with good Dwellinghouse, standing room for thirty head of cattle, Piggeries, Stable, Bacon-curing Room, Tiled Dairy, Straw Yard and Shed, Poultry and Pigeon Houses, Cart and Open Sheds. (now occupied by Mr. Badland).

The Fields comprised in the Estate are in excellent condition, and well supplied with water.

The Property (including the site of the buildings) contains by admeasurement, **37a., Or., 20p.,** or thereabouts.

The Mansion and Buildings are in splendid repair and decorative condition, and are throughout replete with fixtures of an unusually perfect and costly character.   The premises are well supplied with gas and water, and the sanitary and heating arrangements and precautions against fire are of the most complete description.

The Estate, whilst within easy distance of the populous towns and districts of Bradford, Leeds, and Keighley, affords within itself a most charming country retreat of an exceptionally attractive character.

The above Property will first be offered in One Lot, and if not sold will be offered in separate Lots, as follows:

LOT 1.

THE MANSION HOUSE,

Lodge, Stables, Coach-houses, Outbuildings. Conservatories, and Servants' Houses, with the Gardens and Pleasure Grounds,

the site thereof contains **18 acres** or thereabouts.

LOT 2.

THE FARMHOUSE,

With the Outbuildings and Six Closes of Land,

containing, with the site of the buildings, **19 acres** or thereabouts.

According to an article in the *Shipley Times and Express* of 14th October 1893, the house was built from stone quarried on the site and the interior decoration had been carried out at great cost, with the drawing room decorated by Mr J. Aldam Heaton at a cost of over £1,000. There were also numerous outbuildings including a carriage house with space for six carriages, a separate laundry and there was even a model farm with standing room for cattle, piggeries, a bacon curing room, a tiled dairy, and poultry and pigeon houses. (This farm still exists and is situated just below the former site of Ferniehurst School).

There were pleasure grounds round the house which were described as tastefully disposed and planted with forest trees, herbaceous, alpine plants, shrubs, and ferns of all descriptions. They included flower and kitchen gardens, several greenhouses and forcing pits, three vineries, a mushroom house and a gardener's bothy.

The greenhouses were used for growing orchids; Edward Salt had one of the foremost collections of orchids in the country and his Odontoglossum house was considered a model of perfection. According to George Sheeran in his book *Brass Castles* an article in the *Gardeners' Chronicle* described a visit to see Edward Salt's collection of orchids and more particularly a plant of the now well-known Oncidium macracanthum, with a spike 12 feet long bearing forty four flowers! (His brother Titus Salt junior also grew orchids at Milner Field). Eight greenhouses were devoted to their culture and the commercial value of their contents was very large.

There were also large soft and hard tennis grounds. The house itself was situated in an elevated position with a southeast aspect and it would have had magnificent views across the valley to Thackley and Wrose.

According to the sale catalogue "the situation is unique and although in such close proximity to manufactories it enjoys an immunity from all nuisances including smoke".

At this time the Baildon area was very rural and Edward Salt enjoyed the life of a country gentleman (the 1861 census described him as a magistrate, manufacturer and landowner), in his younger days he rode to hounds and he also enjoyed angling and shooting.

In 1861 he had married Mary Jane Susan Elgood (who came from Leicestershire and whose cousin had married Edward's older brother, (Sir) William Henry Salt), but they did not have any children and unfortunately she died, aged only twenty nine, in 1870.

The East window in St John's Church, Baildon was given in her memory and according to William Cudworth it is a most beautiful example of art in glasswork. The figures represented are Faith, Hope and Charity and again according to William Cudworth a more appropriate subject could not have been chosen, "for the late Mrs. Salt was a faithful, hopeful, and charitable woman in every sense of the word". She was buried in the Salt mausoleum at Saltaire Congregational Church.

Edward Salt married for a second time in 1871 to Sarah Amelia Rouse the daughter of William Rouse of Burley. Although Edward Salt was a director of Salts, it was his brother Titus Salt junior who took the more active role in running the company after the death of their father.

However when Titus Salt junior died in 1887, Edward Salt had to become more involved in running the company and, like Charles Stead, mortgaged his house and estate to the Bradford Banking Company as security for the firm.

In 1892, when there were already rumours afoot about the stability of the company, he sold off his collection of orchids, perhaps in an attempt to raise some money. The orchids and other plants were put up for sale by auction; Peter Garnett who lived at Moorville (Burley Woodhead) mentions the sale in his diary "Went to Leeds to buy some orchids that Edward Salt was selling at Heppers and bought 19 for which I gave £7 13s 3d... some of them sold at a high price".

However Edward Salt did not manage to save the firm and lost Ferniehurst, just as Charles Stead had lost the Knoll.

The *Bradford Daily Telegraph* of 2nd October 1893 reported that the Ferniehurst estate would be sold by auction on 9th October and that the sale of the contents would begin on 10th October. The sale was forced by order of the bank and the auctioneer estimated Edward Salt had spent £35,000 on the estate (an amazing sum of money), and asked for bidding to start at £20,000. This failed to produce a response and eventually bidding started at £10,000 (the amount James Roberts was to pay for the Knoll) and slowly crept to £12,500 at which point the house and estate were withdrawn from sale. A report of the failure to sell was carried in the *Shipley Times and Express* of 14th October 1893. It is likely that some of the contents may also have been sold at this time. Peter Garnett mentions the Salt sale in his diary entry for 12th October 1893 "Ellen had gone to Salts sale but had bought nothing as things went so dear".

Three years later, in 1896, George Camille Waud whose family owned and ran Britannia Mills in Bradford (the company was known as C. Waud and Co.) bought the house and estate.

Edward Salt moved down to London in 1893 and later to Bathampton House near Bath.

The employees from Salts were very upset by his departure (he was the last of Sir Titus Salt's sons to be involved in the running of the business) and a group of them travelled down to London to see him and present him with an illuminated address and an engraved casket. This casket was made from solid silver, engraved with carvings of orchids and lapagerias and featured the Salt family crest surmounted with an alpaca. From a report in the *Shipley Times and Express* of 25th November 1893 about the presentation it is obvious that Edward Salt was very upset at losing Ferniehurst and at leaving Saltaire.

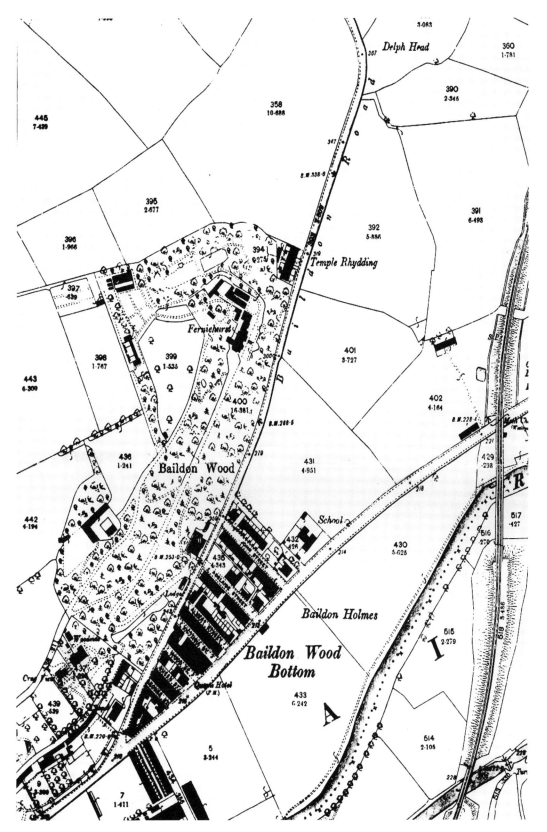

Fig 188: Early Ordnance Survey map detail of Ferniehurst.

167

He had lost everything when the firm was wound-up.

He told the deputation from Saltaire that "I greatly admire and thoroughly appreciate this beautiful casket, which is indeed a work of art. But far above its intrinsic value I place the address, which it contains. Therein I see that, though in other senses of the word I am a poor man, I am rich in having the kindly and affectionate regard of those with whom I have been associated for so many years past. Duty whispered that I ought to go down to Saltaire to receive this beautiful testimonial at the hands of my old friends assembled, but that was an ordeal which at present I dared not face".

However according to his obituary (*Yorkshire Daily Observer*, 27th October 1903) he spent the days of his retirement very happily and in congenial surroundings at Bathampton House, Bath. "The residence is delightfully situated and he was able to indulge freely in what was perhaps his greatest hobby that of gardening. (As at Ferniehurst the Bathampton orchid houses formed one of the chief delights of the owner.)"

Edward Salt died in 1903 and was buried in the churchyard at Bathampton. Unlike his father, Edward Salt was a Churchman and had been one of the trustees for the living of Baildon (his widow died in 1929). Ironically Bathampton House and the orchid houses no longer exist; they, like Ferniehurst, have unfortunately been demolished.

George Camille Waud, who had bought Ferniehurst, was a partner in the firm of Christopher Waud and Co., mohair and alpaca spinners and had entered the mills as a young man and later joined his father, Mr. George Motley Waud, in control of the firm.

In his leisure time he was a breeder of hackney horses and in 1899 he built a hackney training ground and stud at the back of Ferniehurst on what was to become the site of Ferniehurst School. The 1901 census shows that there were a large number of employees working with the horses.

Waud also liked shooting and had a private shoot near Lindley. Also a great rose grower, he was prominently connected with Saltaire Rose Show; indeed, he and Father O'Sullivan of Shipley were said to have one of the rarest collections of roses in the country.

He was also said to be of a very philanthropic nature and to have greatly helped the poor of Baildon.

Waud was also a co-opted member of Baildon Council. While he was chairman of the Council, Bradford sought to incorporate Baildon and there were many stormy discussions on the subject. He was very annoyed when the proposal was successfully opposed.

He was to clash with the Council again when he was selling off the Ferniehurst estate (which, by then, stretched down to Otley Road) and also wanted to dispose of the house itself. Parcels of land were sold off to builders and what had been open country rapidly became built up. The houses around Temple Rhydding Drive and St Aidan's Road all date from this time.

Waud had moved to Caley Hall, Pool in about 1926 and eventually offered to sell Ferniehurst to Baildon Urban Council for the cost of the land alone – an offer he made repeatedly. They declined to take it and so, in about 1932, the house and the surrounding land was sold to a quarrying company.

The house was demolished and the stone from the house is supposed to have been used to build some of the houses on Rockcliffe Avenue.

The lodge which was on Baildon Road near the bottom of Rockcliffe Avenue was left and was only pulled down fairly recently.

After moving to Caley Hall, Waud became a supporter of the Otley Rugby Union Football Club, continued to grow roses (he has a variety named after him) and to shoot.

He died in mysterious circumstances in 1932 as the result of a tragic shooting accident; he had gone out to shoot jackdaws and magpies, according to an article in the *Yorkshire Observer* on 24th August 1932, and was found dead with his gun by his side.

He left a widow and two daughters and was buried at Pool in Wharfedale. Three busloads of workpeople attended the funeral, the firm was closed for the day and the firm's wagon followed the hearse. His name is not forgotten in Baildon as the entrance to the former carriage drive to Ferniehurst is still known as Waud's Gates.

The former site of Ferniehurst and some of the grounds were acquired by Baildon Council during World War Two, after prolonged and delicate negotiation.

The grounds were designated as a recreation area for Baildon. Tennis courts and a bowling green were laid out and a children's playground was built in the lower part of the grounds (which became known as the Dell).

A new entrance was created on Baildon Road and the rather fine gates from the back of Baildon Town Hall were installed. The grounds, like those of the Knoll, were closed at night and were subject to similar regulations.

Some stonewalling, railings and steps are all that remain of the house. The old laundry had become cottages and these were eventually demolished.

The only surviving buildings on the old Ferniehurst estate are the farm and two houses near the site of Ferniehurst School.

Fig 189: The gates marking the current entrance to the former Ferniehurst estate, standing on Baildon Road, now lead into a small, semi-formal park. Neither the gates, the pillars nor their position relate to the original house.

Fig 190: Sarah Amelia Salt, wife of Edward of Ferniehurst, garlanded by orchids, from a portrait by Pre-Raphaelite artist, Frederick Sandys.

A Short History of the Gardens at Milner Field

by Alastair McKinna

Background

In gazing on the Kitchen and Walled Gardens at Milner Field many must have wondered what life was like when such exotic flowers as orchids and lapagerias were commonplace and were being grown there. The Kitchen Garden is now very overgrown but is possibly restorable and one day perhaps we will see the undergrowth cleared and the fields full of vegetables! After all, Helmsley Walled Garden has been successfully restored with Lottery Fund money.

It is exciting that we have here an estate and parklands designed by Robert Marnock, one of the most important exponents of the gardenesque style. In this small corner of West Yorkshire, we have a unique piece of garden design heritage that should be preserved and whose history is interesting.

Introduction

As we have seen, an article on the history of the original Milner Field by Speight appears in his *Chronicles and Stories of Old Bingley* and he notes that on the first Ordnance Survey Map of 1852 an orchard and garden are pictured, roughly in the same position as the walled garden today. Researching further we find that Elizabeth Fell, who died in 1811, aged eighty seven, cultivated the *"fine orchard and gardens at Milner Field"* which *"yielded abundant fruit"* and *"distributed these to the sick and poor at Christmas"*[1]. On the 1852 Ordnance Survey map barely a half mile away is another walled garden and orchard at Gilstead Hall. All signs of this have vanished.

Though Milner Field is now demolished, the park (part of Robert Marnock's landscape design, although now used as pasture,) retains some of its nineteenth century appearance.

Bricks in the ruins of the house show Cliff on their face and were possibly manufactured by Joseph Cliff & Sons of Laisterdyke brick and refractory brick manufacturers (Post Office Bradford Directory).

Milner Field's place in the history of garden design

There were many changes happening in the nineteenth century garden and landscape mirroring the industrial changes that were occurring. J. C. Loudon was perhaps the most significant horticulturalist and influencer, closely followed by Robert Marnock.

The term 'gardenesque' was first used by Loudon in the December 1832 issue of the *Gardeners' Magazine*. Robert Marnock adopted this style in the design of the gardens and the approach to Milner Field; it is somewhere between formality and the informal or picturesque approach.

Writing about the Gardenesque School, Elliott says *"all the trees and shrubs planted are arranged in regard to their kinds and dimensions; and they are planted at first at, or, as they grow, thinned out to, such distances apart as may best display the natural form and habitat of each ... The ideal garden was long established, where the trees have acquired the height of 30 to 40 feet, the shrubberies full and in vigorous health, together with the single trees and lawn shrubs throwing their scattered shade variously over the smooth lawn"* [2].

The gardenesque style required the use of nonnative plants and particular emphasis was given to exotic plants with each plant or specimen being placed for its own appreciation.

Robert Marnock

Robert Marnock was an eminent Victorian landscape designer who was born in Aberdeenshire on 12th March 1800 and died in London on 15th November 1889. It is often claimed, that he was the greatest English landscape designer of his time. Much of his work was in a semi-natural style incorporating areas of flower bedding within the general informal landscape park.

The typical Marnock site was a large villa or small country house in which he dealt with all aspects of the grounds, including siting and management of hothouses and kitchen gardens. Though much of Marnock's landscaping has now been altered or destroyed at Milner Field, we still have a Marnock landscape which needs to be preserved. True, it is now overgrown in parts but with careful management could be restored.

Marnock was influenced by natural forms. His protégé was William Robinson, whose garden at Gravetye Manor he helped to design in his last years. Robinson authored 'The English Flower Garden' which is still in print over one hundred years later and even taught Gertrude Jekyll! Interestingly, there is a Jekyll-inspired border at East Riddlesden Hall a few miles away. Jekyll was known for her contribution to garden colour and cottage garden designs and enjoyed a successful partnership with Edward Lutyens, the architect.

Marnock, together with his apprentice William Robinson, Joseph Meston (who eventually inherited Marnock's practice) and Alexander McKenzie, founded *The Garden* in 1871, the official magazine of the Royal Horticultural Society, which is still published today.

Among Marnock's most important commissions were the gardens at Rousdon, Eynsham House and a parterre garden at Warwick Castle. A list of Robert Marnock's gardens is set out below:

1830	Bretton Hall, Wakefield
1833	Sheffield Botanical Gardens
1839	Royal Botanic Society's Gardens at Regent's Park, London
1840s	Pampisford Hall, Cambs
1846	Sheffield General Cemetery
1850s	Alexandra Park, Hastings
1850	Dunorlan Park, Tunbridge Wells
1853	Villa San Donato, Florence, Italy (home of Prince Demidoff)
1856/60	Berry Hill, Buckinghamshire
1860s	Taplow Court, Eynsharn Hall, Oxon
1868	Rose Gardens and Peacock Garden Warwick Castle
1871	Fairmile Hospital, Oxon (He was paid £30 – £13,000 in today's prices)
1874/5	Weston Park, Sheffield
1870/3	Milner Field, Gilstead
No date	St Michael's Convent, London
No date	Oakes Park, South Yorkshire
No date	Cliveden, near Maidenhead
No date	Park Place, Henley
No date	Sopley Park
No date	Montague House
No date	White Hall
No date	Greenlands
No date	Blythwood, nr Taplow for Mr Geo Hanbury
No date	Rousdon, nr Lyme for Sir Henry Peck, Bart.
No date	Brambletye, nr East Grinstead, for Mr Donald Lamach
No date	Leigh Place nr Tonbridge for the late Samuel Morley and Sir Spencer Wells, Hampstead
No date	Mr McHenry's, Addison Road
No date	Mr Huth, Possingworth
1869	Warwick Castle, Parterre Flower Garden.

He retired from Regent's Park in 1869, some sources say 1862. After this date Marnock gave up his curatorship to practise solely as a landscape gardener. His professional address is given as 11 St John's Terrace, North Gate, Regent's Park. He 'retired' from landscape gardening in 1879 in favour of Joseph Fyfe Meston (born 1827, died 1891), who went on to landscape Hampstead Cemetery.

Marnock first appeared at Bretton Hall, described as Head Gardener, on a list of servants and other employees dated August 1829 when he would have been in his late twenties.

Whilst at Bretton Hall he worked for Lady Diana Beaumont who was very keen on growing exotic plants in her greenhouse which at that time was considered to be the largest of its kind in the world. It was built by W & D Bailey in 1827, cost £10,000 to construct and was heated by steam. This has long since disappeared, but the Camellia House still remains.

During the 1840s he formed a partnership with Mawle, and ran a seed and nursery venture in Hackney. Together the pair sold rare plants for the next ten years as a thriving business.

The *Gardener's Magazine* (23rd November 1889) calls Marnock "*the most talented and successful landscape gardener of modern time*" [3].

Marnock moved on from Bretton Hall when in 1834 he won the competition to design the new Botanic Gardens in Sheffield. Part of the prize was his appointment as the garden's first Curator at a salary of £100 per annum. Marnock had consulted both Decimus Burton and Joseph Paxton in connection with the design of the Sheffield conservatory and in 1839 he won a competition, in partnership with Decimus Burton, to design the gardens of the Royal Botanic Society, laid out in Regent's Park.

He was a regular contributor to gardening and horticultural journals and was editor of *Floricultural Magazine* from 1836 to 1842. From 1845 to 1847 he was editor of *The United Gardeners' and Land Stewards' Journal*, which became *Gardeners' and Farmers' Journal* in July 1847.

Marnock was greatly influenced by natural forms, managing the effect of light and shade. An article in *Country Life*[4], says that Marnock "*helped to promote a form of landscape gardening concerned with making specialised gardens for the fascinating range of new plants being introduced into Britain.*"

Robert Marnock laid out the grounds and park at Milner Field in 1870 and probably also the kitchen garden. Milner Field was reached by a chestnut-lined avenue, now called the 'Coach Road', passing a large fish pond on the left and turning to the left through holly, yew and laurel planting before taking a sharp left through an archway into the courtyard of the house. He fronted the house with a terrace and promenade. By the time you have journeyed from Saltaire, a distance of a mile, the village has disappeared from view and the dark foliage planting of holly, yew and laurel add further screening and create a dark and gloomy atmosphere. This approach, and the planting used, is evidence of the move in landscape design in the latter half of the nineteenth century from pastoral to drama and romance. One can almost imagine Rapunzel lowering her golden tresses from the once derelict North Lodge!

An article from the *Shipley and Saltaire Times* for 1877 records the visit of a party of Keighley Arts Students to Milner Field. "*The spot selected for the outing this year was Shipley Glen; and by the kind permission of Mr Titus Salt, a visit was paid to the beautiful grounds and gardens at his residence, Milner Field. The party numbering in all about three hundred arrived at Saltaire Station by the 1.55 train, where they were met by the Saltaire Brass Band, and headed by the Band, processioned to Milner Field, and afterwards to the Glen."*

The Milner Field sale catalogue of circa 1930 document records: *"Its Winter Gardens and conservatory an enclosure of some 500 square yards, is lofty, well heated and arranged upon the grand style. The semi tropical plants and exotics, which cluster about the marble statuary within its interior, lend an air of almost princely magnificence to the surroundings. The floor of this huge glass enclosed structure is harmonious with many of the other Italian evidences of architecture in the composite whole of Milner Field. It is of carefully designed mosaic work copying the famous Mosaic of the Roman Pavements and villa floors. [...] All around is a wealth of lawns and woodlands, flowers and gardens, shrubbery and rosebeds. There is also a large lake and fishpond spanned in one narrow part by a rustic bridge; a good boathouse is erected on the shore of the lake and there are two or three pleasure skiffs. The stabling and kitchen gardens of the residence are on the Primrose Lane side of the grounds"*.

The dam holding the lake waters back is now broken and the former lake bottom is very wet and overgrown with brambles and rhodedendron. Allan Mirfield, a local historian, recalls a story of a party of men swimming in the lake. When they emerged and dressed there was allegedly one pile of clothes unclaimed: the unfortunate man, it was said, had drowned!

A local resident recalls the swathes of daffodils and narcissi in spring on the slopes leading down to the lake from the Coach Road as late as the 1950s and 1960s. Orchids also grew, but we are unsure of the type.

The outline of the South Terrace of the garden can still be made out amongst the ivy, bramble and briar. The conservatory had a porch opening out on to the terrace leading to garden walks. The view must have been splendid but is now obscured by trees that have grown in the dereliction. The model farm is still viewable from this point.

On the left hand side of the porch there are a number of old roses, now returned to briar. Unfortunately these roses cannot be propagated as they are Canina Major, the common dog rose from which roses are cultivated.

There were steps off the South Terrace down to a small formal landscaped area. This would appear to have been laid out as lawn planted with mature shrubs and trees (Fig 95). The first plans of the garden show two semicircles at either end of this area suggesting formality. These were possibly closely clipped yew, some of which can still be seen today.

Two Walnut trees once stood on the corner at the entrance to Milner Field, just off the Coach Road. It is believed a Spanish Chestnut tree, often used in Victorian furniture, stood in the parkland south of the house. The trees that the Prince of Wales planted in 1882 have proved elusive to locate, as has their 1887 successor.

Close to the entrance to Milner Field, and off to the left, before the archway, stands a magnificent specimen of Evergreen Oak, also known as the Holm Oak, an original 'Marnock specimen'.

The North Terrace, at the rear of the house, is still visible. The steps that led from the terrace on to the croquet lawn remain. The slope appears to have been a lawned area whilst the area between the conservatory and the terrace was planted with roses (Fig 108).

There were a number of greenhouses, possibly as many as twelve, in which were grown eucalyptus trees as well as other flowers and shrubs. However, none of these appear on any Ordnance Survey Maps, but the 1922 sale catalogue has photographs (Figs 39 and 40).

The conservatory was located at the western end of the house and was eighty one feet in length, forty feet wide and twenty six feet high. Tree ferns and palms were located in the centre. There was an Araucaria which reached some twenty feet in height also some dracaenas and aurelias. The Araucaria, otherwise known as the monkey puzzle tree, appealed to the Victorian sense of organisation and tidiness. Young plants were used as centrepieces for bedding schemes. Phormium tenax variegatum could not survive outside (as it does now) but was grown in the conservatory. There was also an old African fern stump Tadea Africana, seven feet high and seven feet across. Lapagerias climbed the roof on the south facing side of the conservatory whilst fuschias and clematis covered the north side. This must have been a truly wonderful sight. A collection of eucalyptus was also to be found in the conservatory. Camellias, the flowers popular with Victorian ladies, ornamental plants and yuccas completed the planting.

The passageway leading into the conservatory was lined with Titus Jnr's 'hobby' plant, the orange tree giving rise to its name "The Orangery". Sir Titus Salt raised banana trees at Crow Nest House at Lightcliffe and, of course, Edward Salt grew his famed orchids at Ferniehurst, Baildon.

This passageway, covered by iron grates (long since disappeared) is still distinguishable in the ruins of the house (Figs 82 and 83).

Titus Jnr took an interest in orchids, as did his brother Edward at Ferniehurst. Edward Salt was frequently visited by collectors and journalists eager to view his collection of orchids.

The choice and type of plants grown were the decisions of the masters of such houses as Milner Field. The head gardener and his team were tasked to raise, propagate and grow a diverse range of plants. They were also encouraged to exhibit at horticultural society meetings. At the Bradford Horticultural Society Exhibition of 1857 Sir Titus Salt's gardener took prizes for heath plants, orchids, black grapes and an orange tree.

The Kitchen and Walled Gardens

The Victorian kitchen garden was a clear demonstration of the prosperous landowning culture of the day. Fascination and fashion for the exotic meant that kitchen and walled gardens and conservatories allowed these plants to be raised and displayed. Several significant developments in the Victorian era allowed glass to become popular.

1845   Glass tax repealed. Larger pieces and quantities of glass were now possible with the invention of plate glass.
1847   James Hartley's sheet glass process made good quality glass available
1850   Tax on timber and brick reduced
1850s   Linseed oil putty became available
1880s   Bessemer's steel process was introduced commercially, allowing cast iron to be fabricated.

Walled kitchen gardens were found in the grounds of most large country houses in Britain and Ireland. There were many such gardens in West Yorkshire, of which only a few remain. The wealth textiles brought to the area was responsible for these country houses, and the abolition of the Brick Tax also accounted for the growth in walled gardens.

Brackets and vine eyes are still in existence on the west facing outer wall of the walled garden at Milner Field showing evidence of trained fruit trees, and maybe peach and grape.

The kitchen gardens were laid out in well arranged plots with herbaceous borders and sanded walks. In front of the walled garden there were ten greenhouses, thirty four feet long and eighteen feet wide, lying due north and south. The paths of the houses are laid with diamond pattern cast iron plates. In the centre of the kitchen garden is the remains of a fountain.

The kitchen garden woodland is a nature conservation area, one of Bradford's wildlife areas. Trench Meadows, (a part of the Milner Field Estate) is now a Site of Special Scientific Interest (English Nature).

The principal houses were laid east to west and entered by a covered corridor laid with three inch thick Yorkshire flagstones. Two houses ran along the back of the 'red line' and five houses either side of the path coming up from the kitchen garden. The 'red line' was a term used to describe the red brick wall that often separated the kitchen garden from the walled garden.

As was usual with houses at this time, the paths of the house were lined with cast iron plates to allow for roots of the vines to pass and for ventilation. The back walls were wired and covered with flowering creepers although we do not know their names. High shelves ran along the top of the walls and strawberries were grown from here.

House numbers six and seven were fitted with pits in the centre, and slate tables around, supported on angle iron rails and cast iron pillars. The tables were covered with small cannel coal which was used as a drainage material and did not become green with algae as did spar and stone. Cannel coal, also known as candle coal, was mined in Lancashire and used as a horticultural product for drainage.

Potting sheds were located at the end of each house. There was a rain water cistern in every house and a hot water cistern (wood) in the boiler house.

On the Sparable Lane side of the kitchen garden are three cordoned pears whilst on the Primrose Lane side are over a dozen apple trees ... which are still fruiting some one hundred and thirty years later! Bradford Urban Wildlife Group has identified some of them such as: Kings Acre Pippin; French Crab (Robin); Grenadier; Newton Wonder; Blenheim Orange; Warner's King, and Bismarck. Very rare lichens on these trees have been identified.

Grenadier was an early cooking apple first recorded in 1862; Blenheim Orange originated in Oxfordshire in the 1740s, first grown by a George Kempster; Newton Wonder was raised in Newton near Derby; Warner's King was developed in the 1700s; and Bismarck, thought to originate in New Zealand, was grown in Germany before spreading throughout Europe.

The name Sparable is a strange one. Two explanations are offered: Sparrow's Bill or small headless nails. This kind of nail was used in buildings where the head of the nail needed to be buried.

Heating and Ventilation System

The houses' ventilation was controlled through handles fixed to perpendicular rods. Some of these are still in place. The heating was supplied by three Weeks patent duplex upright tubular boilers. These are the same type of boiler that were discovered in the restoration of Heligan gardens during the 1990s. The boilers were about seven feet high and were encased in brickwork. Brick vaults were also provided for the necessary supplies of coke or coal, with chutes for delivery. The subterranean boiler house is still in existence but is dangerous with a perilous access point! Some of the heating pipes can still be seen. Valves used in the heating system were two inch, four inch and six inch Peet's patent valves.

Fig 191: One of the overgrown garden bothies.

Pineapple cultivation

The introduction of pineapples to England is generally credited to a London merchant of Dutch origin, Sir Matthew Decker, and they were first fruited by his gardener Henry Telende in 1720. Early cultivation relied on enclosed 'pits' of horse manure one foot deep! The pineapple was very much a status symbol amongst Victorians and Titus Salt Jnr was no exception and in addition to being eaten they were often placed on the dining table as a display and an expression of gracious hospitality.

There were pine and stove pits made with maltkiln ties, about one foot square. The pines grown were principally smooth leaved Cayenne, Queens and Charlotte Rothschild. The mushroom house had to be well built and was usually built of stone and iron and it was situated near to the boilers to maintain humidity. The mushrooms were grown on soil heaped over damp, heavy horse manure.

We cannot know for certain, but the pits in which the pineapple were grown may have been located in front of the Coach House and Stable.

The Greenhouses

One of the houses was dedicated to ferns, in particular a large collection of maidenhair fern Adiantum Cuneatum. Other ferns were Platycerium Grande, Gymmno Gramma and a collection of grasses including Panicum Variegatum.

A house was dedicated to Lapageria Rosea, both red and white forms. Originating from Chile, it is named after Josephine Lapagerie (the maiden name of the Empress of France). The Lapageria Rosea Alba was stated by competent authorities to be "*the best plant of its kind in the kingdom. It extends over a roof space of forty feet, and is said to have borne as many as 4,000 flowers at one time"* [5]. Joseph Dalton Hooker found Lapageria rosea, a beautiful waxy-leaved climber, with drooping bells in red and white, which became very popular in Victorian conservatories.

The *Gardeners' Magazine* says the following of lapagerias: "*In a spacious conservatory, occupying a rather shady position, we have several plants of lapageria rosea and two plants of L. alba, which have done remarkably well, and covered a considerable portion of the roof. Instead of following the orthodox practice of keeping the two kinds separate, the growth has been allowed to intermingle, and the combination of the rose and white flowers is remarkably good; certainly the effect is more pleasing than is the case where only one of the two kinds is grown or when they are kept apart. The flowers of the rose coloured form are most valuable in a cut state, but the blooms of the white form are the most highly appreciated. Indeed our ladies consider them to be the most valuable of all white flowers for dressing the hair, and certainly they have much to recommend them, for they are pure white, waxy in texture, and they stand so well that there is no fear of their fading before the return from the party or ball. The only two points in the cultivation of lapagerias that they may be considered of special importance, are to plant in a border of sufficient size to admit of a fair extension of the roots, and formed with a moderately rich and open compost, and to supply liberally with water, especially during the season new growth is being made. It is, of course, essential to keep a sharp look out for snails when the young shoots are just pushing through the ground, as until they are a foot or so in height the snails have a great liking for them, and do not hesitate to nip off the tender tops if they have a chance"* [6].

The rose greenhouse housed such specimens as Glorie de Dijon and Marechale Niel. These blooms were noted amongst Victorian ladies for their freedom from blemishes and scents.

In the back range of houses were the forcing house, hot and cool orchid houses, melon house, fig house and a mushroom house.

Life in the Backhouses

The Backhouses or sheds formed the garden's working heart as recognised by Rudyard Kipling in his poem *The Glory of the Garden:*

> *"But the glory of the garden lies in more than meets the eye.*
> *For where the thick old laurels grow, along the thin red wall,*
> *You find the tool and potting sheds which are the heart of all.*
> *The cold frames and the hothouses, the dungpits and the tanks,*
> *The rollers, carts and drain pipes, with the barrows and the planks"*

The 'thin red wall' is there at Milner Field and sure enough behind that wall can be found the remains of the gardeners' quarters and potting sheds. Fireplaces can be clearly seen.

From census records in 1881 we have information about the gardeners in Milner Field. Thomas Anderson and his wife Elizabeth (aged thirty-four and thirty respectively) lived at the Gardener's House (now Garden House) with their three children, Maggie, Elizabeth, and Annie Garbutt. The status of the Head Gardener was equal to, if not above, that of the Butler. He/she did little physical labour and was usually provided with a house, fuel and vegetables.

In the Milner Field greenhouses lived five men in their twenties who would have been Under Gardeners. An Under Gardener would earn about thirteen pence a day in 1874, according to records from other Kitchen and Walled Gardens of the period. Their names were Henry Ingham, Tom Tyson, George Black, Francis Allinson and Simon Bulmer. The gardening staff of six would have been an average number for an estate the size of Milner Field.

In 1891 we see only three gardeners employed. They were Thomas Charles Manfield, Alfred Barker and Thomas Anderson.

By 1901 we see a change in circumstances and the number of gardeners increase. William Lamberton is listed as Gentleman Gardener and he lived with his wife Susannah and their children Anna, Fred, Frank, Isabel, and an unnamed son in the Gardener's House. The last two children are listed as Gardener's Assistant and Garden Apprentice. In the backhouses lived three labourers, Tom Cass, George Wray and Mary Wray.

Head Gardeners had a great deal of influence with the lady or gentleman of the house in horticultural matters. Friendly rivalry between the landed gentry through Garden Shows was well known.

Final days and reminiscences

The garden was certainly in use until the Second World War. Robert or Roger Cross ran the garden as a business after the war but sadly he was fatally injured when his shotgun went off as he was climbing a stile in 1957. He is believed to be buried in Nab Wood Cemetery. Roger White, a resident of Cottingley, tells the story that as a child he and friends would climb the wall of the walled garden and shout to Eddie Coonan, one of the gardeners, "Eddie Coonan sells fish three halfpence a dish". Presumably this was a bit of harmless mickey-taking.

The father of local woman Helen Mills was second gardener and he lived with his wife Sarah and their five children at South lodge (better known locally as the 'bottom lodge') in the 1920s. He specialised in eucalyptus trees and flowering shrubs and looked after the conservatory. The lodge was a tied house. It was very isolated and Helen tells how her mother was frightened by men and boys coming up to the woods and they used to have to hide in the house.

Fig 192: The Fountain base in 2009.

Fig 193: Remains of one of the hot houses.

References

1.   Speight, H. 'Milner Field' in *Chronicles and Stories of Old Bingley* (Elliot Stock, 1898)

2.   Elliott, B. *Victorian Gardens* (Springerlink, 1986)

3.   Robert Marnock. (Obituary) *Gardeners' Magazine*, 23rd November 1889

4.   Edwards, P. 'Putting more plants into design' *Country Life*, 16th February 1984

5.   Healey. *A series of picturesque views of castles and country houses in Yorkshire*, 1885

6.   Lapagerias. *The Gardeners' Magazine*, 17th November 1877

Bibliography

Campbell, S. *Walled Kitchen Gardens* (Shire Publications, 2002)

Elliott, B. *Victorian Gardens* (Springerlink, 1986)

Girouard, M. *The Victorian Country House* (Yale University Press, 1979)

Glass Houses at Milner Field, near Saltaire. *The Builder* 25th Jan 1873 p 64

Healey. *A series of picturesque views of castles and country houses in Yorkshire*, 1885

Jellicoe, G., Jellicoe, S. et al. *The Oxford Companion to Gardens* (Oxford University Press, 1991)

Keighley Arts Students at Saltaire. *Shipley and Saltaire Times*, 23rd June 1877

Lee, S. (ed.). *Dictionary of National Biography* (London, 1898)

Milner Field. *The Builder*. 15th March 1873 pp 204-207

Sewell, J. *Marnock's Planting Style and Alexandra Park: Report to Hastings Borough Council*, January 2001

Sheeran, G. *Brass Castles: West Yorkshire new rich and their houses 1800-1914* (Ryburn Publishing Limited, 1993)

Sheeran, G. *Landscape Gardeners in West Yorkshire*, 1680-1880 (Wakefield Historical Publications, 1990)

Stained Glass. *Building News* 5th January 1877

Waterson, E. & Meadows, P. *Lost houses of the West Riding* (Jill Raines Publishing, 1998.)

Appendix 1

Listed below is a list of plants and effects from the Inventory of the Contents of Milner Field, Bingley, made for the estate of the late Titus Salt Jnr in December 1887.

There is clear evidence from this plant list that the Salts, in common with many other Victorian landowners and industrialists, were 'hunting' for plants from the temperate regions across the world mainly America, Australasia, India, South Africa, Japan and China. The Wardian Case (a small portable greenhouse invented by Nathaniel Bagshaw Ward) greatly assisted the Victorian plant hunters in their travels in keeping alive their specimens.

No 1 Vinery : 18 dendrobiums.
No 2 Peach House : 12 small camellias, 15 cutting boxes, 30 dozen geranium cuttings.
No 3 Peach House : 12 cinerarias, 5 acacias, 30 various plants.
No 4 Peach House : 20 chrysanthemums, water barrow on wheels, watering can, 3 dozen eupatoriums.
No 5 Peach House : nil.
No 6 : Plant stove, 240 plants consisting of crotons, dracenias, small palms, allamandas, gardenias, begonias, stephonitas, ixoras, (pancratium), asparagus, cycus revoluta, rhondeletia.
West Corridor : 108 plants consisting of bouvardias, ficus, arums, yuccas, 2 watering cans, portable water engine.
East Corridor : 100 plants viz grasses, cyprus, ficus, bouvardias, watering can, Fitzroys Barometer.
No 7 Fernery : 370 plants viz (a?)ediantums, selginellas, peteris, lamorias, (blechnumrn), davellia.
No 8 Vinery : nil.
No 9 Vinery : 70 chrysanthemums.
No 10 Vinery : coelogynes (orchid), 18 amaryllis, box cuttings, 4 pans lobelias, hosepipe and watering can, 4 rustic baskets.

No 11 : Plant Stove, 80 primulas, 17 chrysanthemums, 30 various ferns, water barrow on wheels.

No 12 Vinery : 2 orange trees, 4 cylognes, 6 various.

No 13 Greenhouse : 320 plants cinerarias, geraniums, humeclegans, margarite, capiscums, mignonette.

No 14 Orchid House : 250 odontoglossums, 20 cyclamens.

No 15 Orchid House : 250 odontoglossums, watering can.

No 16 Warm Orchid House : 70 plants consisting of anthuriums, dendrobiums, cypripediums, cattyleas, 18 baskets.

No 17 Melon House : 20 euchrias, 40 poinsettias.

No 18 Fig House : nil.

No 19 Greenhouse : 109 carnations, 56 azaleas, 20 cytisus,12heaths, 12 eucharis amazonica, 4 pimelias, 2 rustic baskets, 4 bamboos.

No 20 Greenhouse : nil.

No 21 Greenhouse : nil.

No 22 Greenhouse : nil.

No 23 Tomato House : 14 deutzias and prunus, 76 tea roses, 30 primulas, 5 Imantophyllum.

No 24 Rose House : 14 myrtles and cactus.

There are 24 thermometers in the greenhouses.

Appendix 2: Outdoor Effects

Also taken from the Inventory of the Contents of Milner Field, is a list of the contents of the sheds associated with the kitchen and walled garden.

"Top Shed: Snow plough, 2 long trussels, three garden scrays, large snow plough, 2 upright trussels. Old iron and sundries. Bogie, three scaffold planks, Grindstone and frame, iron garden roller, lawn mower, wire trellising, 2 wood stages, 3 spades, 9 iron hangers

Cart Shed: spring luggage cart, hand cart and cover, 3 wheelbarrows, iron ditto, quantity garden sticks. 24 old seed boxes. Six hampers, 4 ladders, old timber

Garden Stable: dun pony, 13½ hands aged, set cart harness, galvanized pail, hay fork, shovel, grip, broom and sundry brushes, galvanised corn bin

Back grounds: 19 frame lights, water cistern, rain tub, garden reel, 2 water tubs, water barrow on wheels, old iron steam piping and bends

Fruit House: Tennis marker, Salters Balance, 6 thermometers, short ladder, pair tennis posts

Gardener's Office: small nest of 9 drawers and sundry tools in ditto, 6 old thermometers, dale rack(?), ink tray and desk sundries. Shell desk, 12 vols on Garden Produce, desk stool, spindle chair, 2 drawing boards, oil can

Pot Shed: Wood bench and vice, sundry joiners tools, 4 spades, 6 wood rakes, 4 iron rakes, 2 dutch hoes, 4 draw hoes, 2 pair edging shears, hedging shears, 2 scythes,

6 brushes, 2 garden syringes, quantity stakes, 500 plant pots off sizes, 6 galvanized pails, pot washing cistern, 3 wire riddles, pounder, 3 iron forks, 2 baskets, 6 watering cans, old lantern.

Coke Shed: hand barrow, ? tools, 2 pair wood steps. Shovel and broom.

Pot Shed No 2 (East): length hose pipe. watering can, seed box, wire riddle and broom, old lawn mower, 50 doz plant pots, old netting, wire fencing, sundry paint cans and contents.

Appendix 3 Milner Field Garden Bank Accounts 1888-1895 (from a note book found among Salt family documents).

1888	295	18	11
1889	483	7	5
1890	459	15	2
1891	537	8	0
1892	431	13	11
1893	377	10	1
1894	348	2	0
1895	269	7	11

It is presumed that these figures are income (though this is not stated).

Fig 194: Presumed staff members outside the greenhouses, the boiler room chimney is visible in the top right corner. Circa early 20th century.